"Everyone in marketing and media in the U.S. needs to understand how to reach and engage U.S. Hispanic audiences, particularly online. No one knows more about that topic than Joe Kutchera, the author of *Latino Link*. Hispanics are the emergent demographic of the U.S., and online is the emergent medium to reach them. **Joe has spent years learning, practicing and perfecting techniques to reach and engage U.S. Hispanics online, and this book shows you how to put those techniques into practice for yourself, your employer and your clients.**"

DAVE MORGAN, CEO, Simulmedia; Founder and former CEO, TACODA and Real Media; Board Member, Interactive Advertising Bureau

"The first rule of marketing is to treat different customers differently. If you assume that consumers are going to change their lives to match your needs, you've already lost. **Joe Kutchera's book is a great place to start thinking about how large communities of consumers are demanding different content from you.**"

SETH GODIN, author of *Tribes* and *Linchpin*

"On the eve of the 2010 Census, CEOs seek solutions for how Hispanics and the Internet can bring new growth to a company's future. *Latino Link* highlights how to connect to Hispanic consumers with culturally relevant, localized content on multiple platforms. **The insights here can help you re-define your brand and business' success in the decade ahead.**"

JACQUELINE HERNÁNDEZ, Chief Operating Officer, Telemundo

"The U.S. Hispanic market presents an exciting growth opportunity for online marketers, especially in the mobile space. *Latino Link* **will help marketers make the most of their online content to attract and retain Hispanic visitors, build their brand presence, and engage this very tech-savvy audience.**"

LISA E. PHILLIPS, Senior Analyst, eMarketer

D1506380

"In *Latino Link*, Joe Kutchera shows companies the enormous opportunity that exists in marketing to U.S. Hispanics online via real-world case studies that make the lessons easy to follow and learn from."

ALBERTO J. FERRER, Managing Partner, The Vidal Partnership

"*Latino Link* is a must-read for marketing and media executives that want to expand their brands into Spanish on the web."

GEORGE HIRSCH, former worldwide publisher, *Runner's World*; Board member, *Salon.com*

"Many of the 30 million Mexicans online use the Internet to plan shopping trips and vacations to the U.S. or simply get the latest news in Spanish and English from their neighbor to the north. **Joe Kutchera is the leading expert in how to monetize this audience and localize your marketing communications content on the web.** His book *Latino Link* provides concise case studies in how to best segment Spanish-language audiences online and develop content for them."

BIANCA LOEW, Managing Director, IAB Mexico

"Advertisers can no longer ignore 30 million online U.S. Hispanics. In *Latino Link*, **Joe Kutchera expertly explains how to use your website and search engines to successfully target your advertising messages in a cost effective manner.**"

JOHN FARRELL, Director, Mexico and US Hispanic, Google

"As digital marketing continues its ascent at the expense of more traditional methods, marketers will also need to realize that Hispanic spending growth will begin to dominate many product categories. Joe Kutchera's *Latino Link* will therefore become **required reading among marketers of all stripes.**"

CÉSAR M. MELGOZA, Founder & CEO, Geoscape

Latino Link

Building Brands Online with
Hispanic Communities
and Content

Joe Kutchera

Paramount Market Publishing, Inc.

Paramount Market Publishing, Inc.
950 Danby Road, Suite 136
Ithaca, NY 14850
www.paramountbooks.com
Telephone: 607-275-8100; 888-787-8100
Facsimile: 607-275-8101

Publisher: James Madden
Editorial Director: Doris Walsh

Cataloging in Publication Data available
ISBN 13: 978-0-9819869-8-2 | ISBN 10: 0-9819869-8-6

This book is dedicated to my parents who met in Spanish class, honeymooned in Mexico, and had me nine months later. I've loved learning to speak Spanish ever since.

Contents

Acknowledgements

"IT TAKES a village to raise a child," the Nigerian Igbo proverb says. The same is true of this book, which required the input and feedback from many experts in the online and Hispanic marketing "village," or industry. Thank you to all of the people mentioned within the pages of this book for your time, experience, and perspective. It is greatly appreciated.

In addition, I would like to thank everyone who helped me behind the scenes to make this book into a reality. These people include:

Jim Madden and Doris Walsh of Paramount Books for believing in this project from the start (and for Doris' patience during the editing and design process).

Carlos Pedraja who brought together much of the research here.

Mariana Chavez for managing my speaking schedule.

Tery Spataro for her insights about writing successful surveys.

Marla Skiko and Pam Daniels for their feedback during my final stretch of writing.

Chiqui Cartagena and Emi Battaglia who provided me with tips for navigating the book publishing industry.

Karen Mac Donald, Laura Mandala, and Rosemary McCormick who provided me with The International Shopping Traveler Study commissioned by Shop America Alliance, Taubman Centers, Mandala Research, and the U.S. Department of Commerce/Office of Travel and Tourism Industries.

Carolyn Petty of Texas Tax-Free Shopping and Denise Thevenot of Louisiana Tax Free Shopping for their insights about Latin Americans shopping in the U.S.

Nina Lentini, my editor at MediaPost, where I first wrote some of the articles that formed the foundation to this book.

Holly McGavock, Monica Gomez, and Jose Maria Alvarez Monzoncillo for inviting me to speak at their respective universities about the ideas in this book.

Alex Banks, Josh Chasin Jack Flanagan, and Joanna Mainetto at ComScore.

Samson Adepoju and Ben Downing at eMarketer.

My dearest family and friends for all of their support while writing this book,

And a big thank you to Ana Grace, Pablo Slough, Nitish Singh, Felipe Korzenny, Cindy Gierhart, Jon Stross and Antonella Severo who took the time to read my manuscript and provide feedback about how to refine my ideas during the editing process.

Last, I would like to thank *you*, the readers, for picking up this book and showing your interest in how to reach Hispanics online.

Introduction

Latino Link: Unifying Audiences through Communities and Content

BIENVENIDOS! Welcome! If your CEO has not asked you how to reach the Latino audience, she or he may well do so in the next six months as business leaders discover that the buying power of U.S. Hispanics will reach $1.3 billion in 2014, growing two times as fast as the general market according to *The Multicultural Economy 2009* from the Selig Center for Economic Growth.

This book aims to help you prepare to reach U.S. Latinos online, as this fast-growing audience has embraced social networks and taps into the many information resources on the web. The first half will educate marketers about how this global medium, the worldwide web, will automatically bring you across borders into new Spanish-language markets since U.S. Latinos often visit Latin American websites and vice versa. The second half of the book offers specific ways to develop localized, culturally relevant content to help you reach your intended market. Some companies may wish to take advantage of the benefits of this global medium especially since the growth rate of the U.S. economy remains in the low single digits, while expanding into Mexico or Latin America means expanding into markets where growth rates approach 10 percent. This can be especially interesting for companies that want to target Mexicans who spend $40 billion dollars *a year* shopping in the United States.

In his book *Imagined Communities*, Benedict Anderson explains how the advent of the printing press, or "print-capitalism," fostered the creation of nation-states where citizens could imagine their fellow countrymen through a common medium even though they could never possibly meet every single one of their fellow newspaper readers. In contrast, the Internet unifies Latinos globally through their common language of Spanish, identity, and common interests. Since business still works within the confines of geographic borders, this book will help you manage this trend and turn your web investment into a success.

So, to start, let's see how two Latinos from Gen Y use the web.

The New Americans: Bilingual, Interactive, Global

In the spring of 2010, while having a lunch of cheeseburgers and milkshakes, my goddaughter Madeline, 11, and her brother Ricardo, 13, asked me, "So, what's your book about Uncle Joe?"

"Well, it's about how families like yours use the Internet and the best ways for companies to communicate with people who speak Spanish," I responded. Madeline and Ricardo speak Spanish with their mother, who immigrated to the United States from Peru, and both English and Spanish with their dad. "What do you two do online?" I asked them. They told me that they spend the majority of their time online on Facebook and MySpace, plus search for things they like on Google, promising to give me a tour of how they use the Internet when we returned to their house.

Ricardo goes online four to five times per week for about 30 minutes per session. Once online, he mostly uses Facebook to connect with his friends from grade school, *capoeira* class (a Brazilian martial art growing in popularity), and his family in Peru. Offline, he likes playing basketball, listening to bands like Linkin Park, seeing friends, and playing video games.

Since she doesn't like playing outside as much, Madeline spends up to two hours a day online on MySpace, where she plays reality games like Sorority Life, and on Facebook, where she chats with her cousins in Peru and Spain. Madeline entered the chat room of one game and asked, "Hola, anyone speak Spanish?" It was very telling. She assumes everyone is like her: bilingual English and Spanish. "Where are the other kids from?" I asked. "All over the world," Madeline told me. To her, the web is a global stage, and we are social citizens, connecting and conversing with others who use the same platforms, enjoy the same games, share the same interests, and read the same news.

As we wrapped up the tour of the Internet, I asked "How much TV do you watch?" Madeline said, "Never"; Ricardo told me, "rarely." That's not to say that Madeline and Ricardo don't watch television content. They do—on websites like YouTube.

If marketers want to reach millennial kids, both Latinos and non-Latinos, they need to develop content—games, videos, articles, tools, and helpful information—and distribute it on platforms like YouTube, MySpace, Facebook, websites, and mobile applications. Just as importantly, they need to *market to* the Spanish-speaking and bilingual Hispanic community online. Truly helpful, interesting, funny, and informative content can attract the right audiences and the best place to do that is on the Internet and on mobile phones.

The most amazing thing about Madeline and Ricardo is that they live in Milwaukee, not in a cosmopolitan, bilingual city like Miami or New York. This is the new Middle America. Kids today can maintain almost daily relationships with family or friends from around the world, even far away places like Peru. This, of course, has enormous ramifications for packaged goods companies, movie studios, and clothing manufacturers that distribute products in Latin America as U.S. Latinos recommend products via word-of-mouth to their family "back home" on social networks.

On a macro level, *eMarketer* reports that 29.6 million U.S. Hispanics, or 59.5 percent of this audience, will go online at least once a month. By 2014, 39.2 million U.S. Hispanics will be online, representing 70 percent of this population. In addition, *eMarketer* shows in its report *Hispanics Online: Demographics and Media Usage* (May, 2010) that the Hispanic market is more receptive to online advertising than non-Hispanics. You can see the growth rate of this audience in the graph on the following page.

U.S. Hispanic Internet Users and Penetration, 2009-2014
(millions and % of Hispanic population)

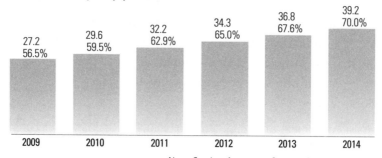

Note: Can be of any race. Source: eMarketer, March 2010

LatinoLink

For further, in-depth demographic research, visit
www.iab.net/us_latinos
to download the IAB's report
"U.S. Latinos Online:
A Driving Force."

Latinos who didn't have access to the Internet five years ago are now online and growing exponentially. This represents an emerging market right in our own backyard. Although Latinos like Madeline and Ricardo spend the vast majority of their time online on English sites, there is still a *lack of content* in Spanish. This presents an opportunity for companies to step forward and provide the information and entertainment that this audience looks for online, especially when the younger generation helps their parents by showing them how to use the computer, search the Internet, and print information from the web. Simmons NCS/NHCS Fall 2009 study confirms this such that 61 percent of Hispanics said, "When I need information, the first place I look is the Internet."

Second-generation, U.S.-born and bi-lingual Hispanics can serve their parents as a "bridge generation," connecting their first generation, Spanish-preferring parents to the information available on the Internet that the family needs to make purchasing decisions. According to the 2010 AOL Hispanic CyberStudy with Cheskin Research, the first and second generation Hispanics together represent 54 percent of online Hispanics and 71 percent of offline Hispanics. Thus, this book helps companies reach three distinct Latino audiences: first and second generation U.S. Hispanics as well as Mexicans who use the Internet to shop online and plan shopping trips to the U.S., which we will learn about in Chapter 4.

Grateful for Content

Marketers can become heroes to Latino consumers in the United States and across Latin America by launching and localizing websites in Spanish or culturally customizing a site for specific geographic regions. This builds trust and lowers buying objections among consumers, making marketers publishers. Marketers start by translating product pages, then "about us" pages, and then customer support content like FAQs or maps to assist consumers in finding store locations. Next, they offer comprehensive translations of a website. Finally, they can offer fully customized websites with a mix of translated and new content with community or user-generated product reviews in-language. Following is a graph from John Yunker, co-founder of the localization firm Byte Level Research, which highlights which content on a localized website will be translated versus user-generated.

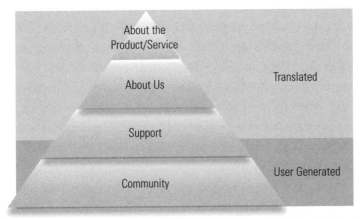

Source: John Yunker, Byte Level Research

When companies get it right, consumers greatly appreciate it. Here are a few examples of consumers' responses.

A reader of the parenting site TodoBebe wrote, "I would like to give my sincere congratulations because TodoBebe is a very complete site that helps moms that don't have the experience of being a mother, moreover when it is all brand new to them. It is amazing that God made the site, that God makes us mothers, which I say because I wasn't able to have a baby and God made a miracle. God bless all of you."

And a BabyCenter reader from Brazil shared a similar story. "I love BabyCenter because it's such a great source of information for mothers. Through the site I realized my baby wasn't developing well in the pregnancy. I was 7 months when I received your newsletter talking about fetal weight. I had an ultrasound to check it and learned she was underweight. So, I had to deliver the baby, otherwise she would have died. Thanks to BabyCenter, everything turned out OK. I'm really thankful. Congratulations to those who make the site, whom, without knowing, saved my daughter's life. God bless your lives."

My Journey into the Latino World

The story of this book begins in 2005. I was working at CNNMoney.com in New York City. At the time, I was taking Spanish classes at Instituto Cervantes in New York and had always been interested in learning about the language, history, and culture of Latin America and Spain. Serendipitously, Time Inc.—the parent company of CNNMoney, *People, Fortune, Time,* and other leading magazines and web brands—saw the growth potential in expanding outside of the United States into Latin America and acquired Grupo Editorial Expansion in Mexico City. An internal Time Inc. email invited its New York employees who wanted to listen to the management team from Grupo Editorial Expansion present the story of its evolution, growth, and why it made sense to join Time Inc. Both sides saw it as a symbiotic opportunity.

It was an impressive presentation, and most everyone who attended nodded their heads in approval. During the Q&A, I asked John Reuter, Expansion's CEO at the time, how the team in Mexico City planned to bring its magazine brands into the digital world. He looked at me and said, "We are going to need people like you to help us figure that out." One year later, in August 2006, I began my new job as Interactive Sales Director at Grupo Editorial Expansion in Mexico City.

Launching CNNExpansion

After a year of intense market research and analysis, in 2007, together with the editorial team we launched CNNExpansion.com, which is now the number one business news site in Mexico and the top Spanish-language business news site in all of North Amer-ica. We built the ad sales from almost nothing to $1 million in 2007; we brought it from being a magazine-only company to become a top-five player in digital in Mexico.

> _Latino**Link**_
>
> CNNExpansion.com

Immediately after our launch, we noticed that while the majority of our site visitors came from Mexico, another 30 percent of our readers visited us from Spain, and even Venezuela and Colombia, markets that generally lack content online. The CNN global brand name obviously strengthened our appeal abroad. In addition, we saw a significant number of visitors coming from the United States. As 70 percent of the Hispanic audience in the United States hails from Mexico, we found, like almost all Mexican sites, that many Mexican-Americans visited the site to obtain news from back home. This process of developing and launching content in Spanish has formed the foundation for this book.

In this book, you will learn answers to questions like:

- How do you translate or create culturally customized content that appeals to Latinos?
- Why do Hispanics leave our country virtually to read news from back home and vice versa?
- Why do Latin Americans visit so many sites from the United States?
- And, most importantly, how can you localize your sites to focus on the exact markets that you intend to reach?

Copy and Reapply

"Good artists copy; great artists steal," said Pablo Picasso. Writers and graphic designers call this "inspiration." In the Internet world, we call this a "mash-up."

Steve Jobs interpreted Picasso's quote by saying, "It comes down to trying to expose yourself to the best things that humans have done and then try to bring those things into what you are doing. . . . We have always been shameless [at Apple] about stealing great ideas. I think part of what made the Macintosh great was that the people working on it were musicians and poets and artists and zoologists and historians who also happened to be the best computer scientists in the world."

This is exactly what I suggest you do. Take the insights, ideas and online content development processes outlined in this book, and then copy and reapply them to your business for the specific Latino audience and geographic region that you wish to attract online.

¿Latino or Hispanic?

Ask three Hispanic marketing experts to tell you the difference between the terms "Hispanic" and "Latino" and often you will hear three different answers. "After looking at polls, surveys, and qualitative studies I have concluded that Hispanic or Latino can be used indistinctly in most cases," says Dr. Felipe Korzenny, author of *Hispanic Marketing* and the director of The Center for Hispanic Marketing Communication at Florida State University.

Some experts interpret the term "Hispanic" as more formal since the U.S. Census Bureau and other governmental agencies use this term to describe people of Hispanic/Latino origin in the United States. In contrast, others interpret "Latino" as more grassroots in that the term originated within the community.

If you compare the definition of *Hispanic* to *Latino* in the Merriam-Webster Dictionary, you see why the confusion arises since Hispanic is defined as, *"of or relating to the people, speech, or culture of Spain or of Spain and Portugal,"* whereas Latino means *"a native or inhabitant of Latin America."* And both words share a secondary meaning of *"a person of Latin-American origin, or descent, living in the United States."*

In terms of their etymology, "Latino" actually refers to descendants of the Roman Empire who spoke Latin, which then evolved into the "Romance" languages of French, Italian, Portuguese, and Spanish. "Hispanic," on the other hand, comes from the name that the Romans gave to the Iberian Peninsula, Hispania, where they spent seven centuries. The name Hispania later evolved into España.

Ultimately, both of these terms are labels, and subject to personal preference. When referring to U.S. Hispanics or Latinos, I use the terms interchangeably as Dr. Korzenny suggests. And when referring to Spanish-speakers pan-regionally across the Americas, I rely on the combined definitions of "Latino" from Merriam-Webster Dictionary: "an inhabitant of Latin America" as well as "a person of Latin-American origin, living in the U.S."

Chapter 1

Soccer without Borders (in an Absolut World)

WHEN Miguel Ramirez and the other founders of MedioTiempo.com started the site in February of 2000, the U.S. Hispanic market didn't even enter their minds. They built Medio Tiempo, which means "half time" in Spanish, for Mexico. Back then, only two options existed for Mexican-Americans to find news about Mexican soccer: the TV stations Univision and Telemundo. Typically, coverage for teams like Chivas, Pumas, or Americas would last only a few minutes during sports shows and possibly be reported by a Colombian newscaster. Medio Tiempo quickly filled that void. Today, 500,000 unique visitors from the United States (according to Google Analytics) visit MedioTiempo.com on a monthly basis, or about 20 percent of its total audience. MedioTiempo.com hasn't invested a cent in promoting the site in the U.S.

"If you make the site appealing to Mexican users and give them the feeling of what it's like to be back in Guadalajara or Mexico City for the game, they will return again and again," says Ramirez. "This shows the importance of good content. The user is one click away from leaving your site."

The U.S. visitors find the site via search and word-of-mouth to get the latest, in-depth news about the teams that they love. Ramirez says this shows two things: the power of the Internet and the enthusiasm of soccer fans. Their user base perfectly reflects where Mexican-Americans live in the United States: 60 percent live in California and Texas. Arizona, Illinois, and New York are home to most of the rest. In addition, its 2008 site survey showed that the visitors were almost entirely young men, below age 40, with over 90 percent of them owning a computer and cell phone.

Comments from the U.S. survey reflect users' passion for soccer and desire to find hard-to-get sports news. Here are two selected comments from the survey (translated from Spanish):

> "I like [MedioTiempo.com] because it's an informative sports site that provides updates about what's happening in the world of sports. I hope that you can continue informing us for a long time about Mexican soccer, especially my team—Cruz Azul. Congratulations for being the #1 medium for sports online. Greetings from Houston, Texas!"

> "Hi, my name is Juan. I am pleased with your site. The news allows me to find out what's happening in the world of sports, without yellow journalism or anything controversial. You represent the positive side of sports with a good, impartial view. My team is 'America' [soccer team based in Mexico City] and I follow their games on cable TV. Thank you for your site and I promise to be one of the faithful followers of your web site. Viva México!"

Looking ahead, Ramirez says that the worst strategy would be to maintain the current Mexico-centered approach. Medio Tiempo, which was acquired by Grupo Editorial Expansion (a Time, Inc., company) in 2008, instead needs to show U.S. Hispanics that it cares enough to develop new products for them. With this in mind, Medio Tiempo will launch a U.S. version of its home page with coverage of Major League Soccer (MLS) events, Mexican National Soccer Team games in the United States, plus its core news about Mexico's soccer teams. The site has also put together a deal with Soccer United Marketing (SUM), which sells its banner advertising inventory in the United States and promotes the site among Spanish-speaking soccer fans. SUM manages the promotional and marketing rights in the United States for Major League Soccer, the U.S. Soccer Federation, the Mexican National Team games in the United States and Club Deportivo Guadalajara [Chivas]. In addition, Medio Tiempo has expanded its popular fantasy league to include visitors in the United States, where they can now enter to win

LatinoLink
MedioTiempo.com

prizes, such as a trip to the World Cup games. Prior to 2010, the prizes were mainly available in Mexico.

If you were to make a heat map of MedioTiempo.com's visitors in the United States, it would probably look pretty similar to the Pew Hispanic Trust's map shown here (with the exception of Miami) since Mexican-Americans make up just about 70 percent of the U.S. Hispanic population.

U.S. Population by County, 2007

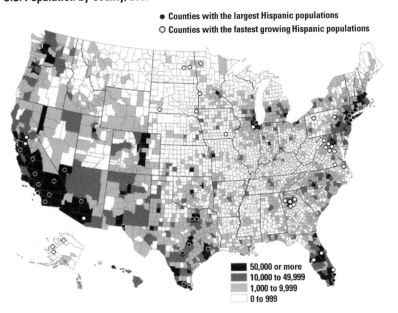

Source: Pew Hispanic Trust

Or better yet, it would look like the maps of the old Mexico since the heaviest concentrations of Mexican-Americans live to the north of the U.S.-Mexico border in California, Nevada, Arizona, New Mexico, and Texas. Prior to the Mexican-American War of 1848, these five states comprised the northern portion of old Mexico, when California was known as "Alta California." Absolut Vodka, with its advertising agency Teran/TBWA, created this "map-vertisement" billboard campaign for Mexico that tapped into Mexicans' desire to return to an "Absolut" (i.e., perfect) Mexico. While the company received a lot of criticism in the U.S., the campaign resonated well in Mexico. Could this indicate that non-Latino's are actually afraid of the Latinization of the United States, to use the term from Cristina Benitez's book of the same name?

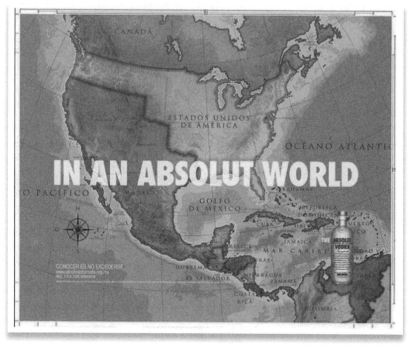

Source: Diageo/Absolut Vodka

Notice the languages in the billboard. "IN AN ABSOLUT WORLD" appears in the foreground in bold white letters in English. In contrast, the proper names in Spanish in the background (e.g., Golfo de Mexico) appear much harder to read. Remember, this ad appeared in Mexico, not the U.S., but it says a lot about the status of English globally. The billboard infers that English is the language of success and sophistication by putting it in the foreground.

In the virtual world, we could say that we already live in the "Absolut" Mexico. At least, Medio Tiempo's visitor traffic suggests that we do. Many Mexican-Americans already live in this larger, virtual Mexico, where they keep in touch with Mexican family, friends, and soccer scores online even though they live in the United States. However much controversy this billboard ad created, it provides a window of truth into the growth of the Spanish-language Internet. Both Mexicans and Mexican-Americans aspire to speak English to "make it," and so using it in advertisements like this one can be effective.

Univision.com: A U.S.-Based Website for Latin Americans?

We know that Mexican-Americans visit Mexico-based sites like Medio-Tiempo.com, but is the reverse true? Do Mexicans visit sites built for U.S. Hispanics? Let's take a look at one of the top U.S. Hispanic websites in terms of unique visitors, Univision.com. Of its 11 million unique visitors (ComScore, September 2009), only 38 percent came from the U.S., 51 percent from Latin America and 11 percent from across the Atlantic in Spain. So the majority of its unique users visited Univision.com from outside of its intended target market. Javier Saralegui, Univision Online's former president, says "We never targeted Latin America for one reason, it was next to impossible to monetize. However, Latin America's online users still found the site, most probably because of Google, a dearth of Spanish-language sites and word-of-mouth." Saralegui and his team also found that the average visit time for Latin Americans was much shorter in comparison to U.S. Hispanics' visit time on the site. Why? The content was culturally customized for U.S. Hispanics and less relevant for Latin Americans, even though it was in the same language.

"There is a clear trend of Spanish-language online media becoming more pan-regional. It started with specific websites delivering content/conversation that was so above the average for the Spanish language that, even if these sites started with a local aim, they ended up appealing to the whole Latin American region and U.S. Hispanics. Many of these local websites were up to the opportunity, and became pan-regional portals," says Jonatan Zinger, director of Search Marketing at Media 8.

Univision.com provides such an example. The trend becomes especially clear when you look at how Univision ranks outside of its home market. While it ranks number 590 in the United States among both English and Spanish-language sites, albeit in an extremely competitive market where Spanish is the second language, Univision holds a higher rank in 16 other Spanish-speaking countries (Alexa, March 2010). It even appears in the top 100 in 12 countries, but not in the United States, the country where it is based!

Univision.com's Worldwide Traffic Rank

Country	Rank
Puerto Rico	29
Honduras	44
El Salvador	49
Dominican Republic	56
Mexico	61
Venezuela	67
Guatemala	70
Ecuador	72
Panama	78
Bolivia	87
Colombia	93
Peru	98
Chile	106
Costa Rica	115
Argentina	179
Spain	273
United States	590

Source: Alexa, March 2010

For a website to build an audience of 11 million visitors, a number of elements have to work in tandem: an editorial team, technology experts, a content management system, search engine optimization, online advertising to drive traffic to the site, and most importantly a well-thought-out strategy. Having a market-leading offline brand helps of course. With Univision's coordinated investment of time and money, especially in search engine optimization, it is no wonder that it has attracted a pan-regional audience outside of the United States that complements the already large U.S. Hispanic online audience. In the chapters ahead, we will learn more about how publishers successfully develop content using the above-mentioned tactics and how this can help marketers and advertisers to evaluate the best publishers for content development and integration.

The Internet's Impact on Acculturation

Michael Melone, who works for the advertising agency Starcom, and his wife, Monica, live in Chicago, where she uses Facebook to keep in touch with family members and friends from her hometown of Pueblorrico, Colombia. "This is a free and invaluable resource for her and her family to share pictures and videos to stay connected," says Melone.

"Yo Quiero a Pueblorrico," Facebook page
("I love Pueblorrico" Colombia, a town outside of the city of Medellin)

Monica also uses MSN video chat to communicate with family members, who make calls from Internet cafes on their end. Some Colombian-American families also shop for their families back home by signing up for the email newsletter of the leading department store, Exito, where they can order online from the United States with an American credit card and have family members pick up products at their local store back in

Colombia. Similar consumer behavior exists for money transfers, according to Melone. Instead of paying high fees associated with companies like Western Union, for example, Colombian-American families in the United States can open an account with a U.S. bank and provide an ATM card to their family members in Colombia. In the United States, they can transfer money into that account, and their family members in Colombia can take money out, as needed. The withdrawal fee is around 5 percent, depending on the exchange rate when the money is taken out. In Colombia, the typical withdrawal fee from any personal account is around 4 percent, so families only pay an additional 1 percent in comparison with withdrawing money from their own personal accounts in Colombia, plus any difference in the exchange rate.

So, how will social networks affect the acculturation process among U.S. Hispanics? The ability to keep in touch with family and friends from countries of origin via email, Skype, and online newspapers back home make it easier than ever. Travel costs are at historic lows. And computer and mobile phone prices fall every year.

Combine this with the fact that more communities like Miami and McAllen, Texas, are reaching the tipping point of becoming a majority of Spanish speakers, and the question about how online media affects acculturation deserves some consideration. Here are five experts' opinions about this issue.

"Latinos have strong ties to their heritage and country of origin," says Alvaro Palacios, the regional director of business development at Terra. "According to Pew's Latino Youth report, only 33 percent of second-generation Hispanics claim to be American first, while 41 percent still prefer to name their country-of-origin. Even with third-generation Hispanics, only 50 percent of them consider themselves American first."

"The Internet is definitely helping with the acculturation process among U.S. Hispanics, with new generations consuming English content on local sites and being almost 100 percent integrated into the U.S. culture," says Marta Martinez, the CEO of StarMedia. "On the other hand, a large percentage of Hispanics consume Spanish sites here and from their country of origin. What the Internet brings to all of us is diversity and choice."

"Being able to understand the culture and institutions in the country they are immigrating to will continue to be important," says Tamara Barber, an analyst at Forrester Research. "But, these different avenues of connecting back home will certainly encourage stronger ties to their countries of origin and could develop into a phenomenon that we see among Hispanic youth, where they are very truly straddling two cultures. The beauty of social media in a cross-border context is that it can actually help immigrants develop more of a bicultural existence."

"Digital technologies have made it much easier to stay in touch with friends and family from wherever they may be; however, I tend to look at acculturation as a choice," says Christopher Stanley, CEO of Alcance Media Group. "If you live in a country for numerous years and need to live and work in the language, 'acculturation' will happen. As a U.S. native living in Chile, I could have easily chosen to surround myself with other non-Latino's living abroad; however, I made the effort to learn the language and culture. Technology may make it more comfortable to stay in a bubble, but it ultimately is a choice."

"Acculturation by definition is not assimilation; it is the layering of native cultural experiences into a new cultural context," says Kevin Conroy, the president of Univision Interactive Media. "In other words, layering in 'home country' experiences over 'U.S.' experiences. This is the reason the use of the Spanish language is still growing (77 percent speak Spanish at home)—Hispanics have not assimilated and lost their language identity. Instead, they have maintained their passion for their language and culture and woven them into their U.S. Hispanic experience. To that end, the web brings value to this dynamic; it enables U.S. Hispanics to more easily stay current with their home country and cultural passion points while remaining very much members of the U.S. Hispanic community."

Lessons Learned

- The new Americans, like Madeline and Ricardo, use global platforms to find games and content and to connect with family and friends.

- Spanish-speaking consumers greatly appreciate translated, customized content online.

- Good marketers copy, but great marketers steal, according to Picasso and Steve Jobs. Copy ideas from your U.S. counterparts in digital marketing or from around the Spanish-speaking world. Reapply those ideas to your state, country, or region in Spanish or culturally customize them in English for U.S. Hispanics.

- Mexican marketers and publishers, like Medio Tiempo, can virtually expand their businesses into the U.S. Hispanic market from Mexico since 70 percent of Hispanics are of Mexican origin and already seek out news, sports, and music content online from "back home."

- U.S. Hispanic marketers and publishers can virtually expand into Mexico, as most already have audiences there.

- Latinos aspire to speak English to "make it" and using it in short advertising messages like Absolut did can be effective.

- Consumers sign up for social networks like Facebook and invite their friends to participate online in order to connect with people who share the same interests or city-of-origin.

The jury is still out on how online media and social networking will affect the acculturation process, but it will be interesting to observe in the years ahead as even small towns like Pueblorrico have a presence on networks like Facebook.

Lexicon Marketing: Building a Branded Social Network for U.S. Hispanics

When José Luis Nazar immigrated to the United States from Chile, he saw firsthand the difficulties involved in learning English and recognized the need for a product that would help Hispanics learn at home in an un-pressured, convenient manner. In 1974, he founded Lexicon Marketing to provide the right tools for Hispanics to learn English by creating an audio-visual course, "Inglés sin Barreras," or literally, "English without Borders." Today, Lexicon is a leading provider of self-study language packages using DVDs, CDs, and workbooks to stimulate all the senses that a learner employs in learning a language. Lexicon's at-home courses come from real-life situations—shopping, visiting the doctor, and looking for a job—focusing on the needs of Hispanics with words, phrases, and idiomatic expressions from everyday life.

Lexicon identifies its target customer as:

- A Spanish-dominant immigrant who has been in the U.S. for over three years
- Usually Mexican-American, with limited English skills
- Aged 25 to 35, married with children, less than a high school–level education
- Has an income level of $40,000 or less and works in construction, restaurants, or service businesses
- Has a credit card and owns his own home
- 30–40% own a computer
- 15–25% use the Internet every day, and 10–20% use it weekly
- 75–85% have a cell phone

During its research phase, Lexicon found that the failure to pass immigration reform has resulted in Hispanics having an overall distrust of the American political process, as well as a loss of impetus to integrate themselves into society such as learning English, paying taxes, buying a home, or opening a bank account. At the same time, it found that the Hispanic customer's use of the Internet continues to evolve. Univision is no longer the sole source of entertainment, and that marketing mobile shows great promise for the right campaign. With regards to the digital divide, Lexicon learned that Spanish-dominant Hispanics under-indexed in computer ownership and Internet usage when compared with Anglos and Asians. However, Hispanics adopt at a higher rate and social networking is a key component of their online experience.

Lexicon launched MundoSinBarreras.com (World without Borders) in May 2009 to bridge the digital divide for Hispanics, providing an educational web portal and branded social network to help them improve their lives through free English language lessons, free access to a board-certified immigration attorney, health and technology channels, and a platform for users to speak up on important socioeconomic issues. The "Dinero" (money) and "USA para ti" (USA for you) channels provide readers with an understanding of the American financial system and available government resources. Overall, the Mundo sin Barreras initiative fits with its aspirational brand and leverages the core competencies of its company along with its vast content base.

> **Latino Link**
>
> MundoSinBarreras.com
> InglesSinBarreras.com

Lexicon developed this social networking site for Spanish speakers with the intention of targeting U.S. Hispanics and found that many Mexicans and other Latin Americans joined the social networking community to make or connect with friends and share their stories about the challenges and successes of learning English. "Our consumers want to have their friends and family join them in the Mundo world, so they tell them about the site," says **Karissa Price**, Lexicon's former vice president of growth initiatives.

During its first year, the site averaged almost 40,000 unique visitors a month. Of those, 70 percent came from the United States, 15 percent from Mexico, and the rest from Latin America and Spain. While Lexicon does not currently localize, or target its content to specific IP addresses, it plans on localizing the site in the future to better meet the needs of sponsors who do business only in certain states or countries.

The response has been excellent. "The feedback we've gotten has been tremendously positive regarding the social networking side of our site," says Price. The site has more than 7,000 registered and active users, most of whom visit it at least twice a week. Because company officials focus on the Spanish-dominant, immigrant population in the United States, they find that consumers need a tremendous amount of information and have a desire to share experiences among themselves. For example, Hispanics need better information about how to navigate the immigration and U.S. financial systems, technology, and health.

Most of all, its consumers want this information from someone they can trust. "The Sin Barreras brand stands for a trusted advisor in the Hispanic community, and our users view the new MundoSinBarreras site as a safe place to get the information they need," says Price.

While Lexicon does not sell software on MundoSinBarreras.com, it does sell it on its Ingles Sin Barreras brand site. In its retail business, it accepts both U.S. and Mexican credit cards and has the ability to do transactions on both sides of the border. Overall, Lexicon has seen a larger online customer base in Mexico, but it has also seen tremendous sales growth in the United States over the past two years. Lexicon's customer service operation is based in Tijuana, Mexico, along with its call and sales center. All of the planning, design, and content was developed in-house while a vendor, Isabeaux, in Peru, manages the programming.

In the years ahead, Lexicon plans to offer more in-depth content in the areas of health, technology, and immigration as well as develop cross-marketing partnerships with select brands and retail partners as it did with Coca-Cola. In addition, it will expand its advertising to television to promote the site, so Lexicon can let a broader audience know about the free tools and content available to them. It also plans on partnering with like-minded educational organizations to further the success of the Hispanic community.

What advice does Lexicon have for other marketers launching a Spanish-language website? "Do your homework and have a clear goal in mind when you build your sites and campaigns," says Price. "Lexicon is fortunate in that we are 100 percent focused on Spanish-speaking customers. We don't have to deal with translation and trans-acculturation issues in our creative process, as we are a Hispanic company serving Hispanic consumers. I would recommend that other marketers focus their online efforts in-language and provide more content for the growing Spanish-speaking community online."

In conclusion, Lexicon has learned that Spanish-dominant consumers are here to stay and are looking for high-quality, life-enhancing products and services to meet the needs of their families. Spanish dominant consumers appreciate being advertised to in Spanish and expect customer service in Spanish as well. Spanish dominant consumers are concentrated in the top 10 DMA's (designated market areas) and yet have spread out across the U.S. into all 50 states. Cross-marketing partnerships with other trusted brands like Coke can help you build brand and drive down marketing costs.

Chapter 2

Findability in Spanish

IN THIS chapter, you will learn how search has created a pan-regional effect with online media and how the "long tail" of niche searches presents an opportunity to tap into consumers' highly targeted needs and wants. Later, in Chapter 10, I will outline specific, tactical solutions for the above-mentioned trends that will ensure that Spanish-speakers find and visit your domestic website, as well as how you can use search engine optimization (SEO) and paid search.

Google Usually Sends U.S. Hispanics to Foreign Websites

Put yourself in the shoes of a bilingual or Spanish-preferring U.S. Hispanic and try searching for something in Spanish on Google, Yahoo!, or Bing. What do you find? Often, more than 50 percent of the results come from sites outside of the United States: in Mexico, Spain, and other Spanish-speaking countries. Let's look at some examples of what appears on the first page of natural (unpaid) results on Google.com when you type in the following search terms (March 2010):

Vuelos a Nueva York (flights to New York): 8 of 10 non-U.S.;

Restaurantes en Los Angeles (restaurants in L.A.): 5 of 10 non-U.S.;

Recetas mexicanas (Mexican recipes): 5 of 10 non-U.S.;

Computadoras baratas (cheap computers): 8 of 10 non-U.S.

However surprising this is, you need to look no further than Google's corporate mission statement to see why it is the case: "to organize the world's information and make it universally accessible and useful." In other words, Google sees no boundaries in the world of information online. Marketers, agencies, and media sellers all work within the economic and political borders of the United States, but search engines index sites globally by language.

A search engine robot ranks results in each language by keyword ranking, the quality of the content, and the number of sites that link to that site (with a preference to sites based within the country's borders). When Google's founders asked themselves what would be the best way to rank search results, they developed their search engine as a virtual super-bibliography. The greater the number of reputable sites linking to another particular site, the higher that site would be listed in Google's results. So, when Hispanics search in Spanish for a niche subject that a U.S. publisher hasn't provided in Spanish, a U.S. search engine sends them to wherever else in the world that content exists online in Spanish: Mexico, Spain, Argentina, and so on.

"El Rey" of the Spanish-Language Content Hill

Spain sits on top of the Spanish-language content hill, having invested US$960 million (670 million euros) in online advertising, according to the 2009 IAB Spain/PWC annual study. The next closest market—U.S. Hispanic—invested less than one-fourth that amount, or about $225 million, according to the *Ad Age 2009 Hispanic Fact Pack*. Many insiders question the U.S. Hispanic number, and believe that the investment could be even lower. In 2009, Mexican advertisers invested $200 million in online advertising revenue (IAB Mexico/PWC annual study), or roughly one-fifth of Spain's investment, even though Mexico's online audience will soon surpass Spain's. This highlights the need for U.S. Hispanic advertisers to invest more in Spanish-language content development and advertising online.

For U.S. Latinos or Mexicans online, it means that when they search in Spanish, many sites from Spain appear in their results, simply because

Spain invests four to five times more in content than other Spanish-language markets. In addition, Spain invests more in website design, usability, and search engine optimization. While Google and its competitors give preference to local sites in search results—so that Mexicans, for example, will be more likely to see results from Mexican sites—many sites from Spain still appear in the results because of the country's larger investment.

This is a double-edged sword. On one side, search engines can send your potential U.S. Hispanic customers to businesses overseas, when they could stay in the U.S. if there were sufficient content here. On the other side, whenever a user searches for a subject like "healthy recipes" and very little content about the subject exists in Mexico, search engines can provide the user with results in their native language from Spain or the United States (or elsewhere). Thus a U.S. company may reach customers from other countries that they would otherwise not attract. In the end though, companies should be aware that their competition for attracting a web audience is global.

How to Redirect Searchers to U.S. Sites

Even though English reigns supreme as the most-used language online, Spanish may surpass English on the global web as computer prices continue to fall and publishers bring more content online in Spanish. New Netbooks today cost around $300, making it much easier for Hispanics and Latin Americans to check email, use the Internet, and call their relatives via Skype or MSN.

The good news amid this seismic change in consumer behavior is the opportunity that this presents to marketing professionals who are ready to try new and more sophisticated ways of targeting Spanish speakers online. In Chapters 8, 9, and 10, I will outline the details of these techniques. But for now, here are some questions to ask yourself and your marketing partners.

- Is your Spanish-language site (or mini-site) optimized for search engines?
- Are you buying country-specific, geo-targeted advertising online

for your search and banner media buys? Or are you allowing your publishing partners to serve those impressions wherever they have Spanish-language visitors across the globe?

- Are you reaching Spanish-speaking U.S. Hispanics via IP-targeted pages on foreign websites through ad networks or exchanges?
- Are you using additional layers of targeting like behavioral, contextual, or language targeting to further segment and understand your Hispanic audience online?

Latino Internet users don't really care about where the sites that they visit are located. They just want the search results in the language that they prefer.

"Search is among the most disruptive innovations of our time," says Peter Morville, author of *Search Patterns.* "It influences what we buy and where we go. It shapes how we learn and what we believe. It's a hybrid between design, engineering, and marketing." Therefore, optimizing your Spanish-language websites for search is crucial to your success.

Reaching U.S. Hispanics on the "Long Tail" of Country-of-Origin Sites

In his book *The Long Tail: Why the Future of Business Is Selling Less of More,* Chris Anderson describes how the digital distribution of music and movies has fundamentally changed consumer behavior when it comes to media. At one point, the "80–20 rule" governed media distribution. That is, "hits" (e.g., Harry Potter, Jay-Z, John Grisham) accounted for 80 percent of a firm's revenues, while "non-hit" items brought in the remaining 20 percent of revenues—even though there were far more non-hits than hits available in the market. The hits just made far more money. Before the Internet, distribution systems and retail channels strongly favored the bestsellers, as shelf space, the number of trucks, and the amount of gas that could be used to deliver products to stores were all limited. But, according to Chris Anderson's theory, the trend has reversed, so that the hits now comprise 20 percent of revenues while the non-hits comprise 80 percent. Anderson refers to this as "the long tail," describing the shape of a graph shown on page 19.

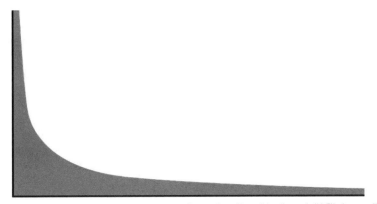

Source: http://en.wikipedia.org/wiki/File:Long_tail.svg

Today, because digital distribution enables vast availability of niche products for consumers, while at the same time requiring negligible stocking and distribution costs for e-commerce companies, the buying behavior of the online population has flipped the 80–20 rule to favor the previously hard-to-find items. Everyone buys something in the long tail, even if it's songs by your cousin's rock band on iTunes. While consumers may buy more Shakira or Juanes songs when compared with other individual artists, collectively the market purchases more copies of "non-hits," according to Anderson's theory.

This concept became a bellwether for bloggers and niche online media companies as they hoped it would mean a chance to edge themselves into the media marketplace next to the Time Warners and News Corps of the world. And in no place did this become more clear than the way we consume media on search engine results.

With this principle in mind, what would you imagine the top *indexing* sites reaching U.S. Hispanics 18 and older who prefer Spanish to look like? A report from ComScore finds that mixed in with popular sites like Univision.com are the Mexican versions of Google or Yahoo!, social networks popular in Latin America like Sonico or Hi5, and the newspaper *El Tiempo* from Colombia. Even sites from Spain like Musica.com or the video site Tu.tv appear as the top indexing sites.

Clearly, as Chris Anderson suggests, search has changed the game in the "distribution" of media. Type "viajes en latinoamerica" into your favorite search engine and you will be whisked away to a site based in Spain without even knowing that you've already left the country! Thomas Friedman was right: The world is flat. Evidently, U.S. Hispanics who prefer to read in Spanish leave our borders via search to read foreign sites for many niche subjects. Univision, Telemundo, Yahoo en español, Terra, and company have competition: global publishers in Spanish.

Eduardo Arcos, founder of the Spanish-Language blog network Hipertextual says, "This is no surprise for me. Hispanics don't care about where the site is from as long as they understand what they are reading or that they are interested in the information they find."

Alex Banks, comScore's vice president for Latin America, says, "The U.S. Hispanic audience does consume a significant amount of Spanish-language content online, with a large portion of this content often coming from foreign countries. Within comScore Media Metrix's February 2010 data, we see that approximately 45 percent of El Pais' global audience, and about 25 percent of Marca's, comes from outside of Spain. Furthermore, for Televisa Interactive Media's sites, we see more than 50 percent of their global audience coming from outside of Mexico." Banks attributes this to the increasing globalization of the Internet. "Over a period of a few minutes, individuals can visit their favorite news site in Colombia, watch video highlights of their favorite Brazilian soccer team's last game, and then wish their friend in Argentina a happy birthday via an international social network. At any moment, any individual can 'virtually' be anywhere they want to be thanks to the Internet."

Hispanics regularly leave our borders to visit foreign sites to stay in touch with the news from their homeland and stay connected with their family and friends, as we saw in the case of Madeline and Ricardo. Latinos can be bilingual and bicultural, and straddle two worlds. They don't have to pick one or the other.

So, what are your options for reaching U.S. Hispanics on these foreign sites within the United States? Planning a buy based on the top 10 indexing sites would be difficult because many of these sites do not have sales representation in the United States. Yet, collectively, they have significant reach with targeted, niche content. The major portals can sell you their domestic Hispanic audience, but that audience is oftentimes found on mid- and long-tail sites, many of them not even based in the United States. Ad networks and exchanges can segment online ad inventory geographically by country, state, or metropolitan area (based on the IP addresses) on these long tail sites and some of them can apply the necessary content filters to ensure that your brand appears in a safe environment.

In Chapter 10, you will find a chart of the Hispanic ad networks and how those partners present opportunities to reach Hispanics on the long tail of online websites.

Lessons Learned

- Search engines foster a global view of information online influencing what we buy, where we go, how we learn, and what we believe.
- Google "organizes the world's information and make it universally accessible and useful," where information is indexed globally by language but also with a preference towards where the content "lives" or what country the content is from.
  - The markets that invest the most in content online (and search engine optimization) will also dominate in search results in Spanish worldwide.
  - Due to a shortage of content in Latin America, Internet users find foreign sites in Spanish via search and, increasingly, via social networks.
- Hispanics regularly leave our borders to visit foreign sites to stay in touch with the news from their homeland and stay connected with their family and friends.

H&R Block: Launch of Spanish-Language Website

By Angela Malloy
Multicultural Marketing Manager
H&R Block

H&R Block launched its first Spanish-language content online in 2005 by offering users "find an office" functionality directly within our English-language site. We then moved into adding content pages in Spanish on its own unique URL.

We soon realized that we weren't doing enough on our site in terms of Spanish-language content and functionality. Plus, we certainly weren't doing anything significant to promote the site. (We never purchased search or display advertising until January 2009.) Before we proceeded to promote the site online via search, banners, and placing the URL on our other sales materials, we knew we needed to make some big changes to ensure the experience was a positive one and that users found the site useful. Our goal was to grow consumer consideration for using H&R Block as a tax preparation company.

As the population of the United States changes, we know that Spanish-language use in the United States will also grow. We've focused on the Spanish-preferring and Spanish-dominant tax filers and non-filers as they represented the largest opportunity for growth. Our target will change as Latinos born here in the United States grow older: second- to fourth-generation Latinos who are bilingual and closely tied to their Latino heritage. That being said, immigrants to the United States who are new to the concept of taxes are more comfortable going through these processes in their native language. We also see that the use of the Internet for finding information has steadily grown. Children, who are

> **LatinoLink**
> www.HRBlock.com/espanol

very comfortable using the Internet, go online to help find information for their Spanish-speaking parents or grandparents for a variety of topics.

Selling an Intangible Product to Hispanics Online

Data has shown us over and over that there is a lack of information on-line in Spanish, especially regarding taxes. When it comes to selling an intangible product, there are definitely challenges for test or trial, especially when this service is only needed once a year. We wanted to work to get our brand, our expertise, and our tax knowledge in front of consumers so that they would consider us a useful resource.

When consumers see you as "the expert" in something, they are more likely to choose you over the competition, especially when audits, refunds, and the government are involved. When consumers find useful information in their native language, they appreciate it and will continue to use the site as a resource.

When we relaunched the site in 2009, we worked to make it very educational and informational. We wanted to provide information about our products and services, while not being *too* sales-oriented. Taxes are a complicated subject, so we offer tax tips, calculators, and descriptions of products and services all in great detail so that our Spanish-preferring clients and prospects could see our expertise and begin to consider and trust our brand.

Targeting Unbanked Consumers: Explaining a New Product Category

We know that many of our Spanish-preferring/dominant clients are "un-banked," so we take a more educational approach with much of our content online as we adapt it for users who know less about the banking system. The Internet is a safe way to get useful information without feeling pressure or fear because we also know many of these clients are distrustful of governments, banks, and corporations.

We offer products such as the "MasterCard prepaid Emerald Card," where you can put your tax refund on a prepaid debit card and reuse the card for purchases. It is an introduction into the concept of banking but without opening a bank account. We also talk about saving for the future, college funds, retirement planning, and tax implications of these choices. It's all safe and free information with no hard sales push. We have to remember that an additional hurdle exists when you speak another language or have moved to a new country. We aim to provide information and educate Hispanic consumers, allow them to review it, ask questions, and then take action. We want to be a partner, not just a service provider.

Translation of the Site

We also don't do a 100 percent translation of copy. We would love to write all of our copy from the ground up, in Spanish (as we do in most of our marketing and advertising); however, the act of filing income taxes in the United States is an American institution, and the laws come from the government—in English. So we are forced to take another approach with a lot of our copy. We look at the English copy developed by our marketing teams and Tax Institute (interprets and manages the ever-changing tax laws from the federal and state governments) and then we decide how we need to "tweak" the copy for a Spanish-dominant or -preferring reader. Some questions that we ask include:

- Do we need to break some things down and explain more since there may be a knowledge gap about taxes or banking?
- Do certain phrases make sense?
- How do we manage the many tax acronyms from the IRS?

When this exercise is complete, we then send it through translation. From here, our vendor, LanguageWorks, adapts the copy to ensure that the essence of the information is relayed in Spanish since we know that many times the same words or expressions just don't work the same way in another language.

Determining What "Flavor" of Spanish

Because there are so many Spanish-speaking people in the United States and many come from different countries and backgrounds, we want to be understood by everyone but also not offend or turn anyone off by a certain word choice or "flavor." We work to use a Spanish translation that includes the most common and proper words, expressions, and verb tenses. This way everyone understands the information—even if it's not exactly the way they might have stated it.

We also have a Puerto Rican website because the tax terminology and local taxes are different. When translating and adapting content for this site, we use the Puerto Rican or Caribbean Spanish term *planillas* in most instances when referring to taxes. We do know that the *planilla* is the actual paper form, not the formal word for "taxes" as a subject, but when people in Puerto Rico talk about taxes, they use the term *planillas*. Because that's what is used on the street, that is the word we use.

We use the term "taxes" in our other advertising media: TV, radio, and out of home. We even use taxes in our online banners. We've done much research and revisit this topic regularly as there are varying opinions of what the correct word is to communicate "taxes" in Spanish. The reason we used *impuestos* on the website is that our English website uses the term "taxes," and, during tax season, a great deal of search dollars are paid for that English term. We didn't want the multicultural group bidding on English terms and starting a price increase. So we went with *impuestos* during year one and ensured that our "En Español" link was clearly visible on the English website for those that use "taxes" when searching for Spanish content, but still ended up on an English site. This year, we decided to use groups of terms like *preparador de taxes* or *preparación de taxes*. We hope to track users who search for "taxes" in Spanish. In addition, we use Omniture's path data to understand avenues that users take on our sites—for example, when and where users move from our Spanish to English sites and vice versa.

Differences Between the Spanish- and English-Language Sites

Our English and Spanish websites may look very similar, but there are some big differences. To name a few:

- We don't offer digital "DIY" products in Spanish, but we do in English.
- We don't have full Spanish experiences for our "Find a tax pro" or "Make an appointment" functions, but we do in English.
- We don't have the community site in Spanish, but we do in English (a blog, similar to Yahoo! Answers).

For these reasons we see users move back and forth between our sites. Some users start on the Spanish site and move to the English site to make an appointment or find a tax professional. We also see users move from the Spanish site to English to purchase online products (DIY). We also see many people come to the English site, then move directly to Spanish, which leads us to believe they want to view Spanish content over English, especially if they stay on the Spanish site for prolonged periods of time.

Most Popular Features

The "Find an office" function is very popular, along with our "Tax tips" page and our calculator to estimate your refund. We offer "Find a tax pro" and "Make an appointment" on our English website, but we do not yet have the resources to make these processes 100 percent available in Spanish. A client or prospect can go to our Spanish site and search for an office where Spanish is spoken, and then find the tax pros in the office who speak Spanish as well as see their experience, credentials, and a short bio. We still see this as a popular feature on the Spanish site even though the experience starts in Spanish and completes in English. Before the process switches to English, we direct users to a landing page where they are informed that the rest of the process will be in English.

Our tax professionals all upload their bios online. With our bilingual tax pros, we ask that they fill out their bios in English and Spanish so that the page still has Spanish information and the experience is as close to complete as possible.

Promoting the Site

The first year we put special focus on promoting the Spanish website was 2009. Previously, the URL had only been communicated via printed materials such as brochures and fliers. Starting with tax season 2008, we ensured the URL was in our TV spots, on the radio, and on billboards. During tax season 2009 we started with a baseline plan to gather information about our target group and their online behavior, their interaction with our site, as well as how we could increase traffic. We chose to move forward with banners and paid search terms. We also put the URL on all materials to really push HRBlock.com/espanol. We don't tie vanity URLs to any tactics for brand continuity. It also helps with ease of memory. For this reason, we can truly track 100 percent of what we do online. So far, the banners drive the most traffic for us as we appear on popular sites such as Univision and Yahoo! en Español. In addition, our media team at OMD Latino has done great work in getting us coverage via roadblocks in financial sections of the sites and headers or border placements on the home pages.

Measuring for Success

We initially weren't sure how to measure success, as we'd never tracked traffic on the site. We weren't promoting the site via avenues that gave us data, and we just started from scratch in 2009 when we decided to promote the website and use Omniture to gather metrics for site traffic. So, for now, our goal is to do better than last year.

We do try to pace in line with our English campaigns and compare ourselves to their programs even though we know it's not apples to apples. H&R Block has been doing online promotion and programs in English *much* longer than Spanish, so if our click thru rates and conversions are anywhere close to theirs, we think we're doing well since we've only been investing in this space for two years. We also like to look at the activities people perform online on our site: finding offices and tax pros or making appointments. We track who moves all the way through these processes on our site, who moves to the Spanish site (remember that "Find a tax pro" and "Make an appointment" are only in English), and when in the process they drop off.

Advice for Marketers Launching a Spanish-Language Website

What do you want Hispanics to find on your site? What is the goal of attracting new customers? Many resources are required for launching a site in Spanish that aren't expensive but necessitate pulling together many people within and outside of your organization: developers, translators, reviewers, QA specialists, strategists, marketing experts, product teams, IT, functionality and usability experts, and ad agencies, some of whom may not be equipped to assist in the Spanish-language work.

Promotion also requires a lot of coordination on many fronts to ensure that you reach your consumer, track the tactics, optimize the site, make creative changes, and maintain consistency with the general market, English site, and campaigns. We wanted to stay in-line with the look and feel of the English and Puerto Rican sites since we believe in "one brand, one voice." However, you must prepare to rethink current strategies and messages and how they may or may not be applicable to the Spanish-speaking consumer.

The process of implementing a Spanish-language website is not as easy as it sounds. People think that, when you have a website in English, you can just translate the pages, create a clever URL, and "POOF" you have a Spanish website. Then you buy a few search terms, maybe get some banners done—and then *la gente* come in droves. It's a lot to think about, and it all has to start with strategy and asking a lot of preliminary questions. Think it through vertically, horizontally, and then shake the snow globe and think again.

Mistakes to Avoid

Luckily we didn't make any big mistakes when relaunching the site or when starting our promotion of the site online. It took a lot more time than we realized, as there is a lot of QA that goes into starting a new site: proof-reading copy, ensuring links work properly, checking navigation, choosing imagery, designing the home page, and so forth. So I recommend preparing for things to take longer than initially expected.

We also had a few small issues with tracking since we didn't ask some of the right questions up front. We made a few assumptions that certain reporting would be provided for the Spanish site since it was available for the English site, but we were incorrect. When setting up the site, there were some technical background issues that kept certain tracking from being immediately available, and we learned to lay it all out on the table up front so we were in the "know" on everything related to tracking.

The only other thing I would recommend *not* doing is to simply translate your copy directly into Spanish without thoroughly analyzing how the messaging and information might need to be refocused based on a different target client. For example, we know that the Spanish language requires more text to explain the same concept in English. We had some pretty copy-heavy pages last year because it's often difficult to explain tax laws without a lot of detail. However, when we changed the design of these pages, we noticed the user would stay on the page longer even though we had almost the exact same copy as last year—the only difference was the design and layout.

Chapter 3

The Great Unifiers on the Web: Language, Culture, and . . . Shopping

"THE medium is the message," Marshall McLuhan famously proposed in his 1964 book *Understanding Media: The Extensions of Man.* By saying this, he suggested that we should focus on the characteristics of a medium, instead of studying the content that the medium transmits.

The worldwide web, as a global network without any boundaries, connects people as no medium has done before, especially people who speak the same language or share the same culture, as we saw with Madeline and Ricardo in the introduction. This chapter will provide an overview of how many Spanish speakers are online, explain why bilingual Hispanics consume media in both languages and discuss how the web can aggregate shoppers looking for electronics, in the case study from Best Buy.

Language Without Borders

Not surprisingly, English dominates Internet World Stats' list of the top 10 languages online to such a degree that you could call the Internet the "English-net," as the majority of users speak English.

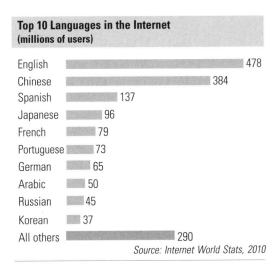

Top 10 Languages in the Internet (millions of users)

English	478
Chinese	384
Spanish	137
Japanese	96
French	79
Portuguese	73
German	65
Arabic	50
Russian	45
Korean	37
All others	290

Source: Internet World Stats, 2010

However, by the time computers, or smart phones, or perhaps tablets cost US$100 or less, the Internet will much more closely resemble the list of top spoken languages in the world, which *Ethnologue: Languages of the World* shows as:

Mandarin	845,000,000
Spanish	329,000,000
English	328,000,000
Hindi/Urdu	242,000,000
Arabic	221,000,000

U.S. Internet Population vs. The Rest of the World

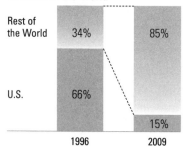

Rest of the World 34% | 85%

U.S. 66% | 15%

1996 | 2009

Source: ComScore World Metrics, July 2009

Note that Spanish is above English. This is important for two reasons. One, it identifies the growth markets and languages online in the years ahead. Two, it highlights the globalization of content online in languages other than English and the diminished market share of the U.S. online. To further illustrate this point, the diagram on the left shows that the U.S. represented only 15 percent of the total Internet population in 2009 compared with 66 percent in 1996 (ComScore). The graph below shows that while U.S. companies dominate the entire top ten list of worldwide properties

Worldwide Top 10 Properties

	U.S. Audience	non-U.S. Audience	Total WW Unique Visitors (MM)
Google sites		80%	597.2
Microsoft sites		80%	545.6
Yahoo! sites		75%	495.3
eBay		71%	249.3
AOL LLC		60%	247.9
Wikipedia sites		79%	242.6
Amazon sites		67%	166.0
Fox Interactive Media		53%	160.6
Apple Inc.		69%	140.3
CNET Networks		74%	125.6

Source: ComScore World Metrics, July 2009

(ComScore), up to 80 percent of their visitors come from international audiences. All have more than 50 percent of their users outside of their home country.

The map below shows the global imprint of the 21 countries that speak Spanish across three continents and five regions:

Europe	Spain
North America	United States, Mexico
The Caribbean	Cuba, Dominican Republic, Puerto Rico
Central America	Costa Rica, El Salvador, Guatemala, Honduras, Nicaragua, Panama
South America	Columbia, Venezuela, Ecuador, Peru, Bolivia, Argentina, Chile, Paraguay, Uruguay

Notice how Spanish has permeated the United States on this map, a trend that many believe will increase over time, especially in the Southwest, Florida, Illinois, and New York. U.S. Latinos' connections to their families and friends in their countries-of-origin on the web, especially on social networks, will naturally bring marketers into Latin America. Because of our proximity to the region and its parallels to the Hispanic market, it will present new business opportunities.

Source: Wikipedia—Hispanophone World Map

Rank of Spanish-Language Markets

Internet World Stats shows that Spain holds the top spot for Internet users but that Mexico will soon surpass Spain as the number one Spanish-speaking market as its online population is growing much more quickly. If we rank each Spanish-speaking country by its online growth rate, we see that the emerging markets are truly expanding, as we do in the graphic below. The Dominican Republic, Paraguay, Guatemala, and Equatorial Guinea all have grown more than 2,000 percent in the last 10 years. Spain is just a little button on the bottom of the circle! If we could indicate the U.S. Hispanic online audience (Spanish-preferring and bilingual speakers), it would hold the number three position in the world, above Argentina and behind Mexico.

Spanish-language markets ranked by rate of growth, excluding the U.S.

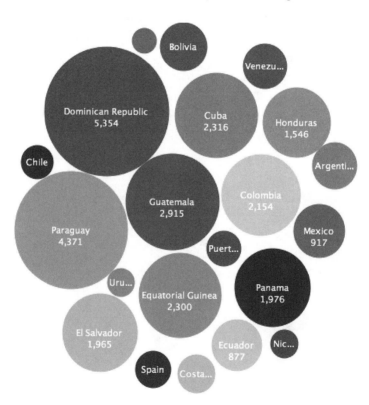

Image source: Internet World Stats (data) and IBM's Many Eyes (visualization)

In-Culture or In-Language?
From the Perspective of a Bicultural Hispanic

Bicultural Hispanics often switch back and forth between Spanish and English. To learn why, **Elizabeth Perez**, the Digital Insights Analyst at ImpreMedia, describes why she chooses content in English or Spanish based on the cultural and political orientation of the news in each language. In-Language media is simply written in a consumer's native language whereas in-culture media provides news from the perspective of the viewer's native culture.

As a Southern California native born in Ventura County to Mexican immigrant parents, I, like many of my peers, grew up speaking Spanish until I went to elementary school, where I learned English. I enrolled in a bilingual educational program where I learned to read and write in my native language, Spanish, and English until the fifth grade, when I switched to classes in English only. From that moment on, until today, I continue to speak, read and write in both languages.

Media Coverage of U.S. Immigration Reform:
My Thoughts about How I Use Media

After graduating from college, I enrolled in Baden Powell Institute located in Morelia, Michoacán (Mexico). While living there, I learned about Mexican history and lifestyle. My move came at a time in which the U.S. citizens became very active and reacted to the illegal immigration reforms by voicing their views and participating in public street rallies. "The Great American Boycott" took place on May 1, 2006, and ended in a violent attack in Los Angeles, where police officers shot rubber bullets at the protestors marching in MacArthur Park.

I was studying in Morelia and followed it closely by reading my hometown's daily newspaper online—*The Ventura County Star*—and *La Opinión*. Every day I logged online and started visiting sites such as ABC, CNN,

Univision and Telemundo, which offered online video clips covering the latest news on the reform. I also started reading blogs and comments about the reform, which, for the most part, were full of negative, even racist, comments. I felt the urge to voice my opinion (all the way from Mexico), and the only way I was able to do that was by commenting on blogs and debating with those who were also blogging.

After moving back to the United States and completing my classes in Mexico, I watched the coverage on TV—mainly Univision and CNN. Additionally, I continued reading online and blogging. There was a sense of separation amongst those who were either for or against the reform. It became clearer as I noticed the difference in reporting between the Spanish- and English-language networks. The main difference of course was the audience the networks were reporting to.

The Spanish-language networks spoke to Hispanics and were mainly pro-immigrant. The English-language networks spoke to the general market that for the most part was anti-immigrant. I continued watching and reading about it through both Spanish- and English-language media outlets to stay informed. However, I consumed more Spanish-language media as I felt I related to it more. I also felt they went beyond reporting the news to inform and educate their audience about legal rights and places where they could seek help. In addition, being Hispanic myself, I couldn't help but feel a personal connection and a need to support my community.

This was one of those moments that I really appreciated being bilingual. I was able to navigate from one media outlet to another despite the language and get the perspective on both sides of the debate. On one of my visits to LaOpinion.com while I was reading an article about the reform, I noticed a section that read "Jobs at *La Opinión*." I clicked on the icon and found they had a job opening that really interested me. After reading the description, I sent my resume over, and about two to three weeks later, after going though the interview process, I was hired. Nearly four years later, I still work for ImpreMedia.

Writing from a Non-Hispanic Perspective Viewed Differently
There is a bit of an odd feeling obtaining news about Hispanics from non-Hispanics. Sure, a non-Hispanic can report the news, but how much of what they are reporting do they understand or even care to learn? For example, if non-Hispanics were to come to a Mexican birthday celebration,

they may be horrified to see that, after we sing "Happy Birthday" or "Las Mañanitas" to the person celebrating his or her birthday, we chant "que le muerda! Que le muerda! (Bite it! Bite it!)," and, as the person bites the cake, we push him or her into the cake.

A non-Hispanic might wonder why we would do that or think that we ruined the person's party by doing this. However, in reality, that is part of our tradition and one very much looked forward to. You would not know about this unless you were exposed to the culture. For reasons such as these, when I have the option to obtain news coverage about Hispanics from a non-Hispanic or Hispanic media outlet, you will more likely see me turn to the Hispanic media outlet, as it will be the one I will relate to the most.

However, that doesn't mean that I won't consume non-Hispanic media. I would simply choose whichever one I felt gave me the most relevant content to what I'm searching for. The great thing is that, nowadays, it is very easy to jump from one media outlet to another and compare content with the Internet.

In-Culture News While Living In-Language

To further understand the relationship between in-language and in-culture media, let's go to a country where they speak Spanish to see how Latin American immigrants seek out the media they want. With 1.5 million Latin American immigrants from countries such as Ecuador, Peru, and Argentina in Spain, you would think that the local media would satisfy their information and news needs since both the Spaniards and the immigrants speak the same language, but that's not the case. The Latin Americans in Spain find little local in-culture news or information tailored to their needs—for example, news about Ecuador's soccer team, South American celebrities, or economic news about how exchange rates will affect their wire transfers back home.

Because of this, many immigrants visit websites from their home country. In fact, the demand for in-culture content, also in Spanish, from the Ecuadorians and Bolivians proved so great that *El Comercio de Ecuador* and *El Correo de Bolivia*, the two major daily newspapers in their respective countries, opened offices in Madrid to distribute print versions of their newspapers and began to bulk up their reporting online. The "natives" hoped to "conquer the motherland."

Two Retailers, Two Routes

In Chapter 4, we will explore the subject of cross-border shopping, focusing on how much Mexicans spend in the U.S. and why. But now, let's explore the inspiration for this book: a comparison between two retailers that launched Spanish-language websites for U.S. Hispanics, both of which discovered that many international visitors found the site. One shut its site down (the wrong choice) and the other made it into an opportunity. Not only do language, culture, and news connect people but consumers finding high quality products at good prices does as well.

The Home Depot vs. Best Buy

In early 2009, The Home Depot launched its Spanish-language e-commerce site for U.S. Hispanics, "a replicate of the English language e-commerce site, with 40,000 products available to online shoppers," according to the company. It hoped to reach a new audience and grow a new profit center. After only four months, The Home Depot shut the site down because many of its visitors came from Latin America and Spain. The site was set up to accept only U.S. credit cards. Nevertheless, Spanish-language consumers located outside of the United States clearly communicated their interest in online home improvement content and e-commerce by visiting The Home Depot's U.S. Hispanic site.

Because The Home Depot has more than 90 stores in Mexico, many Mexicans already knew the brand and easily found the site via search. They were surely pleased that the retailer was "speaking their language" online. Unfortunately, The Home Depot's organizational structure (U.S. versus Mexican business units) clashed with the international, borderless nature of the Internet, and its U.S. Hispanic e-commerce venture failed. In essence, the U.S. e-commerce site was competing against the Mexican business unit because middle-to-upper-class Mexicans online in Mexico found the site just as easily as U.S. Hispanics did. According to Leonard Wortzel, The Home Depot's multicultural manager, The Home Depot hasn't given up on the Hispanic customer; it's just that the timing wasn't right and the resources weren't adequate for a site of that nature at that time," according to a statement on Juan Tornoe's blog, May 21, 2009.

Best Buy is a completely different example. When Best Buy launched its U.S. Hispanic e-commerce site, also in Spanish, it found the same consumer behavior online as The Home Depot had. Many visitors from outside the United States visited the site. In contrast to The Home Depot's decision, Best Buy embraced visitors from Mexico and Latin America, encouraging them to buy online with foreign credit cards and to pick up merchandise in-store when they visited the United States. In addition to generating e-commerce sales, the site also helped Hispanic consumers become more informed about purchases they wanted to make in-store. Best Buy associates reported that many U.S. Hispanics printed out pages from the site and brought them into the store, so they had a better understanding about what they wanted.

Win–Win vs. Lose–Lose

How could one retailer so completely embrace one of the greatest benefits of the worldwide web—its global distribution—and create a U.S. Hispanic and international e-commerce success story while another rejected it?

Best Buy created a win–win situation by building sales with U.S. Hispanics and Spanish speakers internationally. The Home Depot, on the other hand, lost not one but two e-commerce opportunities by cutting off service online both to U.S. Hispanics and Latin Americans. **Chuck Whiteman** of MotionPoint, a website translation, hosting, and globalization company with clients like Best Buy, Victoria's Secret, Delta Air Lines, Domino's Pizza, and The Home Depot's Hispanic site says, "It's pretty clear to us that the world is becoming a global marketplace. We see a lot of companies reaching out to the Spanish-speaking market first because it happens to be both a domestic and an international market. Once they see the demand from outside the U.S., they quite frequently start looking at a more comprehensive global strategy that goes beyond Spanish."

Consumers Always Want Lower Prices and Good Quality

In addition to e-commerce sales, retailers with stores along the U.S.-Mexico border know that many Mexicans shop in the United States for groceries and especially high-ticket items. With higher taxes and less competition, prices in Mexico are noticeably higher.

Compare prices for identical products on Dell.com vs. Dell.com.mx, and you'll see why Mexicans cross the border to shop: Dell's Inspiron 15 notebook on Dell.com in the United States costs $549 (with the following features: 4GB DDR2 at 800MHz, Windows 7, 320GB hard drive). The Inspiron 15 on Dell.com.mx in Mexico, with lower-quality features (2GB DDR2 at 800MHz, Windows 7, 250GB hard drive), is priced at $9,999 pesos—or, at 12.20 pesos to the dollar, $819 U.S. dollars (comparison made March 2010).

Because of higher taxes and less competition in Mexico, buying an Inspiron 15 Dell laptop with the *better* features in the United States will cost $270 less than it would in Mexico. Online consumers will always compare prices to find the best deals and even go so far as to travel to the United States to buy them. The web will only bring greater transparency to the shopping experience globally in the years ahead.

Chris Emme, director of sales for Yahoo en Español, says, "I know when relatives or friends of my wife, Leticia, are visiting because boxes arrive at my apartment from the Gap, J.Crew, Disney, and Amazon. My wife's family and friends from Argentina find that the bargains and quality of products in the U.S. far exceed the products they can buy in Argentina." Millions of other consumers shop like Leticia's family and friends.

Emme continues, "Since most sites require a U.S. address to ship to, we get all the deliveries. So when they come to our apartment, we load them up with all their goodies and they bring them back home and dispense them accordingly.

"As funny as it sounds, my wife and I actually participate in this practice as well. We live in downtown Manhattan and have a car parked nearby so every couple weeks we head over to New Jersey to go grocery shopping," Emme says. He finds that both the selection and prices are better. In addition, he always fills up his gas tank because that is much cheaper as well. So while he pays a toll to come back into Manhattan (about $8), he saves close to $50 to $75 on the groceries and gas, not to mention saving himself the aggravation of grocery shopping in the Big Apple.

By listening and responding to the millions of visitors to U.S. Hispanic websites from abroad, you can turn your international website into millions of dollars of new e-commerce business.

Tips for Growing E-Commerce with U.S. Hispanics

Ask your colleagues the following questions to grow your U.S. Hispanic e-commerce revenues:

What percentage of your domestic U.S. Hispanic sales actually come from Spanish-language foreigners like Chris Emme's wife or Mexicans crossing the U.S.-Mexico border?

Do you measure international sales among Spanish speakers via credit card statistics or couponing programs?

How can you promote your e-commerce site or physical stores virtually to strategically grow sales along the U.S.-Mexico border?

Do you have Spanish-language customer support in-store or on toll-free numbers to provide sufficient follow up service with your customers? Do your toll-free numbers work outside the U.S.?

Do your store associates speak Spanish?

Do you measure in-store sales based upon consumers doing research on the web and then coming in-store to make a purchase? Hispanics new to the Internet may feel less comfortable making purchases online with their credit cards. In Mexico, for example, e-commerce, mail delivery systems, and credit cards have historically not been trusted to the degree that they are in the U.S.

Do you have a "welcome mat" or pop-up window for international visitors on your U.S. website funneling them to the right pages for international sales?

Lessons Learned

- The English-net may dominate the Internet today, but languages like Spanish and Mandarin present the best growth opportunity. Most likely, the Internet will look like the top natively spoken languages in the next five years, especially as computer prices fall and mobile phones become more common.
- Many of the emerging markets' Internet audiences in Latin America have grown at more than 2,000 percent in the last 10 years.
- Many bilingual Hispanics consume media in English or Spanish, not because they have an easier time understanding one or the other, but because they feel the news reporting has more relevance to them.
- By expanding our web presence into new languages, don't forget that everyone else in the world can find you.
- Listen to what consumers want. Think beyond traditional boundaries. Figure out how to accept international credit cards. Take what someone else considers a failure and turn it into a success.
- The web will bring greater transparency to shoppers globally in the years ahead, especially those who compare prices between markets.

Best Buy en Español

***By Ana Grace
BestBuy.com Site Manager,
Hispanic Initiatives & Online Catalogs***

Background and History

Best Buy's broader efforts to serve the Latino customer began modestly by having employees wear name badges identifying them as Spanish speakers, printing our weekly ads in Spanish in a few key markets, and creating a Spanish landing page on our website, which provided translated legal policies but largely linked to English content on the BestBuy.com site. Not an ideal-customer experience overall. Based on feedback from our store associates and customers, we knew we needed to provide a better experience for our Spanish-preferring customers. We had to authentically and holistically embrace this market, and, to do that, Best Buy needed to start by speaking Spanish. Our new value proposition? To offer an end-to-end, in-language research, shopping and purchase experience across all channels. Call, click, or visit.

Road to a Spanish Website

Research indicated a growing demand by U.S. Latinos for an in-language e-commerce consumer electronics experience. In an early 2007 report, a major research company validated the feedback we had been getting from our store teams. They suggested that companies like ours should consider launching a Spanish-language website in order to reach out to the growing and largely untapped Spanish-language market.

Our core hypothesis for translating the site was that, as products and solutions become more complex, customers will need to be able to read about them, compare them and purchase them in your

LatinoLink
Espanol.BestBuy.com

preferred language. Given the size of the opportunity and based on feed-back we were receiving, Best Buy decided to launch a parity (mirrored) version of our English website in Spanish.

Like many online retailers, we faced the unique challenges of man-aging a large, very dynamic site, which was loaded with time-sensitive information. This made the idea of translating BestBuy.com into Spanish a complicated project, especially from an IT perspective. We had three issues to overcome:

- IT development and integration costs
- Keeping pace with the rate of product and promotional content changes
- Launching the site in the narrow window between our holiday seasons

We identified a third-party firm with proprietary technology that enabled us to build an end-to-end parity Spanish e-commerce experience in 87 days without involving our IT department. The Spanish website launched in Sep-tember 2007, just in time for the holidays. We translated more than 12,000 products, including all items in the areas of TVs, computers, cameras, ap-pliances, phones, MP3s, and we are continually adding new content to the site. Notably excluded were music, movies, and third-party content.

A Learning Philosophy

Best Buy went into this market with the full admission that we had a lot to learn about the Latino customer. Our founding principles included:

- Our customers are diverse in origin but common in their basic desire to be understood and to understand their technology.
- We are prepared to test all our assumptions and to listen to our customers. The Latino customers are telling us what they want; we just need the willingness to listen, learn, and act.
- We consider this a long term relationship with Latinos in the U.S. and are committed to learning and growing along with them.

Traffic

"If you build it . . . they won't come." We learned that you can't just launch your site in Spanish and hope that the Latino market finds it. In fact, for three years, we actually trained our customers *not* to click on the Spanish link because all that we had to offer them when they got there were Spanish legal policies and Spanish links to English content. We realized that we needed to relaunch the site as a new entity and aggressively communicate to our Latino customers that this is a parity online experience, identical in quality and security to our English site. We are still experimenting and learning how to communicate this change to our customer effectively by using all our marketing levers, including traditional (TV, print, radio, outdoor), digital (web, social and mobile), and internal (store signage, employees) resources.

We also found that our employees make the best ambassadors for the Spanish site. They are in an ideal position to drive customers to the website by increasing awareness and encouraging consideration. Additionally, customer satisfaction surveys indicate that customers who learn about the Spanish website through our store employees are more satisfied with the Spanish online experience overall.

Time on the Site

Our Spanish-preferring customers spend roughly double the amount of time on the Spanish site as compared with English-preferring customers on the English site. We theorize that this is the result of limited detailed product information being available elsewhere in Spanish on the web, and thus our Spanish-preferring customers are really engaging with the content on the Best Buy website.

Average Order Value

Our Spanish-preferring website customers' order value is about double what our English-preferring customers spend online. We believe that our hypothesis is playing out and that Spanish-preferring customers are researching (and ultimately buying) their more complex purchases on the site, and this is resulting in a higher average order value on the Spanish site.

Conversion

The visitor-to-sales conversion rate on the Spanish website is just under what it is on our English site. Latinos report that, while they enjoy shopping and buying in our stores, they do much of their research online. We believe that this phenomenon is at work here. The Spanish site is a strong driver to the stores with some stores reporting that their Latino customers are bringing in printouts from the Spanish site to show employees what they want.

Toggling

We have noticed that some of our customers are toggling back and forth between the Spanish and English site. When we asked them why, some said they wanted to compare the two translations or went to the other site seeking clarification. Another segment of customers indicated that they wanted to be sure they were getting the same deal on the Spanish site as on the English site.

Building Trust Through Content Parity

Our initial assumption was that, in order to attract and engage our customers, we would need to provide unique content and offers on the Spanish site (e.g., develop product bundles, graphics and/or experiences we thought would be attractive to this customer). Before we did this, we wanted to validate our hypothesis. We conducted a usability study (observing people navigate and use the Spanish website), and we were surprised to find that, instead of unique content, what they adamantly wanted was an experience that was the same as the English site. Differences in offerings and even in imagery created fears of discrimination and broke down trust. Based on conversations with customers and the data we gathered, we concluded that our original hypothesis was in fact invalid for Best Buy. As a result, we shifted our efforts toward creating a unique and compelling invitation as opposed to creating unique site content.

Satisfaction

A customer satisfaction survey is offered in Spanish on the Spanish site to those customers who visit the site. Scores are significantly and constantly higher on the Spanish site compared with the English site. The trend in the satisfaction numbers has held over two years, since the launch of the site. We believe that our Latino customers are giving us credit for being leaders in the Spanish e-commerce space.

International Demand

When international customers (customers with a non-US IP address) come to BestBuy.com, they are greeted by a welcome page, which invites them to select a language and informs them about our ordering program for international customers. This welcome page has increased our international visits to the Spanish website by over 500 percent. In the future, we will be geo-targeting unique messaging for visitors of different countries both through the welcome landing page and also as they interact on the site.

Although we have many site visitors from the United States, we are experiencing a 2:1 ratio of international to U.S. visitors, primarily from Latin American countries. Best Buy's global brand recognition is high, and visitors from all over the world are interested in the products and services we offer. We recently launched a very successful online program that allows our customers with international billing addresses the ability to order online and either ship their purchases to a friend or family member in the United States or to pick up their purchases at a U.S. store when they are in the country. This has increased revenues as well as customer satisfaction from our international customers.

Cross Channel Support: 360 Approach

As part of a holistic, integrated approach, we are pleased to see that the Spanish website is used as a tool by each of our distribution channels to further our relationship with our Latino customers.

Using the Site in Store

In our stores, customer and employees are able to access the Spanish site through a kiosk and this is a great way to provide our Latino customers with an in-language experience in markets where we have few Spanish-speaking employees. Employees are:

- Using the site as a translation tool to communicate with our Spanish-preferring customers when there is not a Spanish employee available to assist.
- Printing out our product detail pages and providing them to customers to reference during their visit.
- Using printouts from the Spanish site as a type of "take home" product brochure (which are often not available in Spanish).

Customer Support Center

In order to serve both our online and retail customers, we have Spanish call centers in both the United States and Latin America. We also support our online customers with *click to call,* which allows customers to enter their number online and have a Spanish-speaking customer service associate call them back, and are working on developing Spanish online chat. Additionally, we maintain a Spanish community forum, which is available for customers to ask questions and interact with our customer service team. Our Customer Support teams use our site to direct Spanish- preferring customers to the site for detailed product information.

Measuring Success

We look to holistic measures to understand our success. We measure all the traditional online metrics (traffic, revenue, close rate, average ticket), but we also look to our store performance as we know that we are driving sales to our stores. Additionally, we look at brand preference tracking tools, customer satisfaction surveys, and feedback provided through our customer service channel as indicators of what is working and not with respect to this in-language experience.

2010 and Beyond

We plan to continue connecting with our Latino customers around their passion points. Digital and social media will play a significant role, as will connecting on a local level. We are aggressively pursuing opportunities in both the online and mobile spaces, given that our core Hispanic customers have a higher propensity to use these platforms. We are investing as a company in making information available to our Latino customers how and when they want it.

Advice for Other E-commerce Companies

Don't make assumptions about what you think is important to your customers. Get the data, and use it to guide your decisions. Don't assume that language is the complete solution. Language is part of the foundation that will allow you to better serve your Latino customer, but there are elements of lifestyle, culture and core needs that are equally important considerations in this work.

You may not need a Spanish website if you are targeting English-preferring Latinos. In this case, a culturally relevant English campaign aimed at inviting Latinos to consider your company may fit the bill.

When targeting Spanish-preferring Latinos, consider if you need everything translated or just the more complex products. Be aware that translating too little can make the site irrelevant and not communicate that you are committed to the Latino customer.

Consider the parity question. Will you have a mirrored site, a completely different experience for Latinos, or a hybrid of the two? Conduct usability studies and focus groups with your target customers to understand what they prefer. Remember the trust factor.

How will you invite customers to your site? This is a place to be very culturally relevant, and parity seems to be less of a factor. Your banner ads, targeted emails, search campaigns, etc. will be key in driving traffic to your site. Consider the roll of traditional marketing vehicles and emerging marketing tools like social and mobile.

Chapter 4

$40 Billion in Spending from the "Invisible Shoppers"

IN THIS chapter, we will analyze how much Mexicans spend while shopping in the U.S., the consumer behavior of three of these "invisible shoppers," and the size and growth opportunity of the Mexican e-commerce market. According to "The International Shopping Traveler Study," Mexicans spend the most on shopping when compared with the four other top inbound travel countries to the United States—Canada, Germany, Japan, and the United Kingdom. Take a look at their findings:

The 2009 International Shopping Traveler Study

	Spend Shopping	Total Trip Spend	Shopping % Overall
Mexico	$1310	$3249	40%
Japan	$1200	$4722	25%
Germany	$1085	$4127	26%
UK	$968	$3845	25%
Canada	$757	$2490	30%
Average	$1063	$3692	29%

Source: The International Shopping Traveler Study was jointly developed by Shop America Alliance, Taubman Centers, Mandala Research and the U.S. Department of Commerce/Office of Travel and Tourism Industries.

Residents of Mexico outspend those from all other countries in terms of total shopping dollars spent ($1,310 per visit) and percentage spent on shopping (40%) for their overall trip. These findings may not conform with your perceptions of the average Mexican. The Mexicans who live in Mexico often differ greatly from the immigrant Mexicans in the United States in that the ones who leave Mexico, generally speaking, come from the poorest classes while the ones who stay in Mexico are typically better off. Out of a population of 106 million, we can identify six different "Mexicos," the top three of which constitute the target shopper in the study.

	Annual Household Income, in U.S. dollars
The Mega-rich	2.5 million Mexicans: $130,000+
The Upper Class	9.5 million Mexicans: $40,000 – $130,000
The Middle Class	22 million Mexicans: $16,000 – $40,000
The Lower Middle Class	15 million Mexicans: $10,000 – $16,000
The Lower Class	27 million Mexicans: $3,500 – $10,000
The Poor	27 million Mexicans: below $3,500

Source: ESIGMA

Mexicans spend $40 billion annually on trips to the United States, according to Jennifer Stefano, CEO of Border Billboard, citing aggregate numbers from Scarborough Research and chamber of commerce studies. The 206 million people (Bureau of Transportation, 2008) who cross the border from Mexico into the United States every year (including repeat visits) increasingly represent a critical piece of revenue for retailers in California, Arizona, New Mexico, and Texas.

As we saw in Chapter 3, well-to-do Mexicans shop in the United States to get better prices and often better quality products. The study learned other things about Mexican shoppers. For example, they were much more likely to say that family and friends were the reason for their visit (51% of respondents), unlike their Japanese, German, British, and Canadian counterparts, who said, on average, that shopping was a key reason for their visit. This indicates that Mexicans are much more likely to have personal connections in the United States, when compared with the other countries in the study. Stefano, the CEO of Border Billboard, says Mexicans cross the border for a variety of reasons, usually accomplishing a couple of goals during each visit, including seeing family, shopping, going to work, getting medical attention, and even driving children to U.S. schools. So Mexicans were the least likely to say that shopping was the key reason they visited the United States (40% of respondents).

As you will see in the stories that follow of Fabián, Alejando, and Alfonso, Mexican shoppers mix visiting family and friends with shopping during their visits. Two of the top destinations are geographically close to Mexico (Los Angeles with 27 percent of respondents and Houston with 23 percent), although The Big Apple lured just as many Mexican shoppers as L.A. did. And lastly, Mexican shopping travelers took, on average, 4.4 international trips per year.

Some of the other findings from the study highlight how these shoppers are not your "average Mexicans" but rather from the top three classes, as outlined on the previous page.

Mexican Demographics
The 2009 International Shopping Traveler Study

Household Income (percent)

$75,000—$99,000	25%
$100,000—$124,000	13%
$125,000—$199,000	21%
$200,000+	16%
Not sure/rather not say	26%

Note: Total is over 100% due to rounding.

Length of Stay (percent)

Day Trip	2%
½ Days/1 overnight	6%
3–4 days	25%
5–6 days	25%
7–10 days	25%
11–14 days	7%
15+ days	11%
Median	6%

Note: Total is over 100% due to rounding.

Lodging (respondents with overnight stay, percent)

Hotel / Motel / Resort	66%
Family or friends	28%
Bed & Breakfast	2%
Rental home / condo	4%
Owned home / condo	8%
Recreational vehicle	1%

More than one response allowed

Top 10 Brands Shopped for (percent)

Nike	24%
Gap	24%
Abercrombie & Fitch	17%
Levi's	14%
Sony	13%
Polo Ralph Lauren	12%
Tommy Hilfiger	11%
Armani	11%
Calvin Klein	11%
Banana Republic	11%

Source: The International Shopping Traveler Study was jointly developed by Shop America Alliance, Taubman Centers, Mandala Research and the U.S. Department of Commerce/Office of Travel and Tourism Industries.

To paint a profile of these Mexican shoppers, let's take a look at three shoppers who regularly make trips to the United States to shop.

Shopping in the U.S.

Fabián

Fabián, a 33-year-old marketing professional, and his wife of four years live in Mexico City and are expecting a baby soon. When he visits the United States, he typically stays with family members but sometimes stays in hotels.

"I travel to the U.S. about three times per year in part because I have family there, so the main motive isn't shopping," says Fabián. "Nevertheless, I take advantage of the prices and discounts on items that in Mexico would cost two to three times more money."

Typically, he finds that he saves around 50 percent to 70 percent by shopping in the United States in comparison with shopping in Mexico. During a typical visit, he spends around US$3,000 including plane fare, rental car, and meals. He uses the Internet to plan his trips and to find out everything about the city that he's visiting: the tourist attractions, how to get around, store locations, special sales, and products he is interested in. For specific categories of items, Fabián typically visits stores like:

- *Clothing:* Banana Republic, Gap, Polo, Lacoste, Anne Taylor, Perry Ellis, Eddie Bauer, Adidas, Nike, and Brooks Brothers
- *Kids:* Carters, Babies "R" Us, and The Children's Place
- *Department stores:* Walmart, Target, JC Penny's, Macy's, and Neiman Marcus
- *Electronics:* Best Buy, Sony and Fry's
- *Home:* IKEA and Crate and Barrel

A typical day begins at a restaurant like IHOP. "My favorite breakfast buffet when I go to Las Vegas is at the Hotel Paris!" Upon finishing breakfast, he and his family begin shopping. "If it's a day dedicated to shopping, we go to the major outlet malls or one of the main shopping streets like the Magnificent Mile in Chicago."

"If we are just taking a stroll, then it depends upon the city we are in, so, for example, in California or Orlando, we wouldn't lose the opportunity to go to Disney World or Sea World. Or if we are in Las Vegas we make a point of walking up and down the strip and gambling in one of the new casinos. In San Diego, we like to visit the Seaport Village or the Coronado hotel."

Alejandro

Alejandro is 30 years old and lives with his wife and baby in Aguascalientes, Mexico, about 300 miles northwest of Mexico City. As a CPA, he earns a good living and travels to the United States once a year. He spends about US$500 per visit on shopping, and finds that he normally saves around US$1,000 for his and his wife's purchases. In other words, some products cost three times as much in Mexico. "We stay in a hotel during our visits, almost always with the same friends with whom we make the same trip every year."

"The only incentive for going is the price. If the same prices and variety of products existed in Mexico, I would definitely shop here at home. We use the Internet to plan our trip and see what the costs are for the toll fees and gasoline," Alejandro says.

"On our shopping day, we have breakfast at the hotel and afterwards we head to a nearby mall or outlet center. We normally visit shops around the same mall including Toys 'R' Us, Target, Radio Shack, The Home Depot, Carter's, Nike Store, Athlete's Foot, Oakley, Levis, and American Eagle. Recently, the items that we've most often purchased have been for our baby such as clothing or electronic items. This year, I plan on buying an LCD screen and a laptop. When I go with my dad, we look for fishing equipment that is hard to find in Mexico. Or, when it is available in Mexico, it typically costs two or three times more than in the U.S."

Alfonso: Shopping for Baby Valentina in Texas

Alfonso Garcia-Moreno is 38 and was born in Mexico City to a middle-class family. He traveled extensively with his two brothers, parents, and grandparents when he was younger. He and his brothers have master's degrees from top universities in the United States, and he works as an engineer. He and his wife, Elia Mary, recently had a child, Valentina.

"My salary, savings and family support allows me to have a full-time maid, a driver and a 2,500 sq. ft. apartment in one of the best areas of Mexico City," Garcia-Moreno says.

"After living eight years abroad in Italy, I realized it was a tremendous opportunity to try to create a better story about my country, Mexico. You also learn how twisted people's image is about Mexico or the stereotypical image they have in their mind." Garcia-Moreno says many think of Mexico as a "poor country with rancheros with sombreros moving around on burros."

"In Mexico, there are only a few options to go shopping. The lack of competition sets the environment for high-margin retailers and overpriced goods. We also have super fancy high street shopping malls, as any First World country, where local people shop, but you end up facing high prices, a limited product offering, and you seldom find a real sale."

Alfonso's Baby Shopping Experience

"Last year, my wife and I learned we were pregnant. We joyfully celebrated and started to make plans for Valentina's arrival. Obviously, we also realized the financial impact it would have to buy all the stuff a baby, and the mother, needs. "With many lists of products on hand from friends, doctors and downloaded from the Internet, I saw that it would take a big effort to get the best deal on every single product, but it was worth researching the biggest items."

Alfonso traveled to McAllen, Texas, to visit his brother-in-law where he bought all of the baby furniture that you see in the picture at right, plus most of the baby clothes in the closet on the other side of the room. Even with the flight and shipping costs, he still saved hundreds of dollars, plus he had the opportunity to visit family and take a mini-vacation. For example, Alfonso bought the nightstand with the lamp (in the photo) for $20 from Target, whereas in Mexico it would have cost at least three times as much. He calls Mexicans such as himself "invisible shoppers," because they represent such a massive market with tremendous growth potential, and yet very few companies actively target them. That is where the web presents a great opportunity for marketers to reach Mexicans

who search for products and stores in the U.S. and make plans to take shopping vacations there.

The demand from the Fabiáns, Alejandros, and Alfonsos of Mexico has grown to such a degree that you can now find services such as ShoppingFromMexico.com, which enables Mexican consumers "to shop safely and comfortably from Mexico in whichever part of the United States."

If you look at the age of the Mexican shoppers from "The International Shopping Traveler Study," Alejandro (30), Fabián (33), and Alfonso (38) all fit into the two most important age groups, as shown on the graph on the next page.

Age of Mexican Shoppers Visiting the U.S.

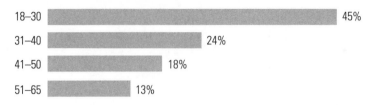

Source: The International Shopping Traveler Study was jointly developed by
Shop America Alliance, Taubman Centers, Mandala Research and the
U.S. Department of Commerce/Office of Travel and Tourism Industries.

In total, according to the study, 69 percent of Mexican shoppers visiting the United States are below age 40, which shows two things. One, Mexico's "baby boom" is coming of age right now. And two, these middle- to upper-income, young shoppers use the Internet to obtain information they need, especially for shopping, and are more Internet savvy than their parents' generation. It's no accident, then, that the graph above looks similar to the graph below, which shows Internet users by age in Mexico. In fact, 78 percent of Internet users in Mexico are below age 34. This new generation of Mexicans grew up with the Internet and used it in their studies at university.

Internet Users in Mexico, by age, 2007
(percent of total)

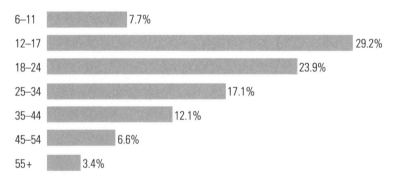

Note: an Internet user is a person of any age who uses the Internet from any location at least once
per month. Source: Instituto Nacional de Estadística, Geografía e Informática (INEGI), "Encuesta
Nacional sobre Disponibilidad y Uso de las Tecnologías de la Información en los Hogares, 2007."
eMarketer, May 17, 2008

Macy's Attracts Shoppers Visiting the U.S.

Macy's launched VisitMacysUSA.com in February 2010 to reach foreign shoppers who visit the United States to find better selection and prices in comparison with their home countries. Macy's plans on translating the site into Spanish because it sees so many shoppers from Mexico each year. The retailer's research estimates that 15.7 million Mexicans visited the United States in 2009, and 87.5 percent of them shopped. (*Source: Department of Commerce and Department of Homeland Security*). The company keeps a close eye on site traffic, downloads of the visitor savings pass voucher, plus any tour groups that reach out to Macy's on its website. Macy's long-term strategy for its travel and tourism services is to continue building and growing the site and to explore marketing and partnership opportunities.

Macy's regularly advertises in Mexican newspapers in border cities like Monterrey, Reynosa, Nuevo Laredo, Juarez, Tijuana and Mexicali. In addition, Macy's also does some broadcast advertising in key border cities. Looking ahead, Macy's will spend more time targeting Mexican visitors by partnering with convention and visitors bureaus that target Mexican visitors, such as Texas, California, the city of Las Vegas, Florida, and New York, plus Continental Airlines. With these organizations, Macy's will go on sales missions to Mexico to meet with major tour operators and travel agents, as shopping provides a key incentive for Mexican shoppers to travel to cities like Los Angeles, New York, and Houston.

Savings + Status = Utility

Price isn't the only reason Mexicans shop in the United States. It appears that, in addition to the cost savings, some Mexicans go for the aspirational benefits of buying clothing or electronics that are not available in Mexico. Most likely, the prestige and status of owning something that is unique plays a part in the decision-making process.

Meeting the Needs of Latino Consumers

John Battistoni, Las Vegas district manager for Best Buy, estimates that
30 percent of the Las Vegas store's sales come from Mexicans and Brazil-
ians who visit the United States and shop for laptops, digital cameras,
and GPS systems. Best Buy meets the needs of these foreign shoppers by
offering laptops preconfigured in Spanish or Portuguese and GPS systems
preloaded with maps of foreign cities like Mexico City and Sao Paulo.

How Much Do Mexicans Spend in the U.S.?

Estimates vary widely as to how much money Mexicans spend in the
United States, in part because little research exists about the subject
but also because most Mexicans make purchases with cash instead of
using credit cards. Kenn Morris, CEO of Crossborder Business Associates,
says, "50–70 percent of cross-border visitors from Mexico do so to shop,
spending US$110 to $160 per trip. In San Diego County, we found that
cross-border shoppers from Tijuana spend US$500 to $600 per household
during the Christmas season." Morris estimates that 18 to 20 million
Mexicans cross the border into the United States every month, representing $25 million to $30 million in daily retail sales along the border region
during normal times of the year. This equates to about $10 billion dollars
annually, but he cautions that it does not include capital expenditures like
cars, houses, or even computers, nor does it include Mexicans' spending
on flights into the United States or holiday spending. Morris and other
experts report that the vast majority of Mexicans pay with cash on their
shopping trips as most Mexicans do not have credit cards. VISA's *Tourism Outlook: USA* from June 2009 confirms this, showing that Mexicans
spent $2.5 billion in the United States in 2008 and $2.4 billion in 2007
on VISA credit cards, considerably below Morris' estimate. (The lack of
adoption of credit cards in Mexico stems from the 1994 financial crisis,
where after the peso was devalued, most Mexicans lost faith in financial
institutions and their federal government.)

Texas' tourism bureau estimated that 6.3 million Mexicans visited
the Lone Star State in 2008, the largest international inbound market

of travelers due to its proximity. Mexico contributes almost half of international shoppers' spending in Texas or $2.29 billion according Texas' Tax Free Shopping, Ltd., a company established to promote international shopping tourism in the state. This equates to $1,576 per visitor who actually claimed a tax refund through its service. My survey of media executives in Mexico City confirms the degree to which Mexicans shop in the U.S. as well. Among the 76 percent of respondents who had visited the U.S. in the last three years, 89 percent shopped during their visit, with nearly 40 percent of those spending $1000 dollars or more. In addition, 34 percent of respondents have shopped on American e-commerce sites. (See the Appendix for the full results.)

The Mexican Commuter Shopper

Twenty-six official border crossings line the U.S.–Mexico border, each with 20-plus lanes of traffic in each direction. With an average wait time of 45 minutes, it surpasses the average commute time of both California and New York City.

Toni Banuelos, Hispanic marketing manager for IKEA, says, "The Tijuana consumer is important to our San Diego store, and having the opportunity to influence their purchasing decision as they sit idle at the border is a key factor to driving our business from Tijuana." Toni says that IKEA asks consumers at point-of-sale for their zip codes. For foreign consumers, IKEA enters a special code for non-U.S. residents. "We know from that data that 7 percent of our consumers in our San Diego store come from Mexico, although we conservatively account for an extra 3 percent because of additional sales at the self-serve kiosks, plus some Mexicans use a U.S. post office box or a zip code from their American relatives."

As the penetration rates of digital media increase, Mexican consumers will have more tools at their fingertips to compare prices online, enabling them to plan and rationalize trips to the United States based on price or tax savings. Still, with Internet penetration at 35 percent and mobile penetration at 80 percent today in Mexico, retailers can develop IP-targeted media campaigns in Mexico or CRM programs for Mexican consumers who shop in the United States via email newsletters and text messaging coupons.

Sun, Sand and Shopping in Miami

More than 17 million tourists traveled to Miami in 2008, according to the Greater Miami Convention & Visitors Bureau in its annual visitor profile and economic impact study (Synovate, May 2009). Of those visitors, the greatest increase came from international visitors, which saw a 5.4 percent increase over 2007 and made up 48 percent, or 5.7 million, of all those staying overnight. The majority of international tourists to the Miami area originate from Latin America, which saw an increase in visitors in 2008 (3.7 million) compared with 2007 (3.5 million). South America accounts for nearly 2.5 million of those coming from Latin America. While more than half come for vacation, this group has declined over the past few years. Now, more visit Miami to see friends and relatives, especially international visitors, one-third of whom said that shopping was one of their most liked activities. They averaged US$230 per visit. In comparison, only 10 percent of domestic visitors identified shopping as a reason for their visit.

E-Commerce in Mexico

To further understand the issue of cross-border shopping and how the Internet has or will affect consumer behavior, look at research from the Mexican Internet Association (AMIPCI), the country's leading e-commerce organization. According to a 2008 study, Mexicans spent $1.7 billion on e-commerce purchases, a growth rate of 85 percent over 2007's $955 million in sales. Interestingly, 79 percent of total dollars spent on business-to-consumer e-commerce comes from plane tickets, mostly because of the incentives that national airlines offer on their sites and also because there are no delivery costs for tickets.

You can see in the graph at right that international e-commerce sales jumped dramatically from 5 percent in 2007 to 14 percent in 2008. So, cross-border comparison-shopping appears to be on the rise. It's important to note that while international e-commerce sales jumped, the entire Mexican e-commerce market grew year over year by 78 percent in 2007 and 85 percent in 2008 from previous years.

The Mexican Internet Association data shows e-commerce spending in millions of U.S. dollars for 2006, 2007, and 2008, divided into:

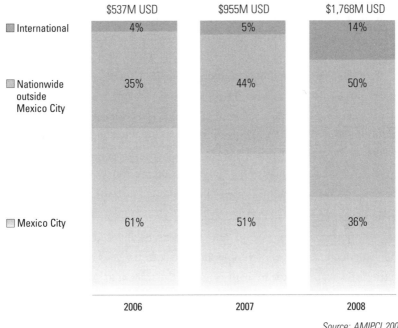

	$537M USD	$955M USD	$1,768M USD
International	4%	5%	14%
Nationwide outside Mexico City	35%	44%	50%
Mexico City	61%	51%	36%
	2006	2007	2008

Source: AMIPCI 2008

Google Mexico's online retail study (September 2009) found that 97 percent of the 3,117 18+ consumers interviewed had purchased a product online in the past six months. Fifty-two percent of them had finished university. Their average age was 32, and their average annual salary was US$19,730. The average number of years for buying online was 2.6. Veteran online shoppers (3+ years shopping online) had a higher level of university education (63%) when compared with those with little or no experience (40%). Also, veteran online shoppers had almost double the spending power of those who had not shopped online (US$25,852 annually versus $13,567).

The main attributes for Mexican shoppers going online were prices, selection, and ease of purchase. The Internet was by far the most used by this Internet-savvy audience—based on days on average and hours per day among all media vehicles, including TV, radio and magazines/

newspapers. In total, Google found that 250,000 searches about retail-related items are performed in Mexico every month.

However, with the total number of Internet users in Mexico jumping from 30.4 million in 2010 to a projected 43.2 million in 2014, according to *eMarketer*, retail-related searchers should increase significantly in the years ahead.

To answer my questions about cross-border shopping and media consumption, I called Francisco Ceballos, the country manager of Mercado-Libre Mexico, the leading e-commerce platform in Latin America. Founded in 1999 with headquarters in Buenos Aires, MercadoLibre is listed on NASDAQ and is 18.5 percent–owned by eBay.

> **Latino*Link***
>
> MercadoLibre.com

"The Internet by its nature is global," says Ceballos. "As long as you know the language, you can access any website from any place on earth. As content is created more and more by users, as opposed to corporations, then the need to have content classified by country goes away." He points to the InFocus projector in front of us on the table and says, "If someone in Spain, Argentina, or the U.S. writes a review in Spanish about this model that can help me make a decision about what to buy, that's all that matters to me."

Because of this trend, Ceballos says MercadoLibre developed a two-tiered approach to globalizing for the web.

Twelve separate websites offer products by country because of the "friction" of physical products going through borders, including duties, taxes, and shipping costs. Nevertheless, many of the products from the sellers, like electronics, originate from China. In MercadoLibre's newly opened markets like Costa Rica, they have a virtual presence but no office yet, as their goal is to build scale while offering free listings.

For user-generated content, the company launches forums internationally in Spanish, so that any of its Spanish-language markets can leave comments. When users search for reviews about specific products, they can find them, crowd sourced, from other users who already own the product.

Ceballos admits that his competitive set includes not only the retail and online stores in Mexico, but also the big online players in the United

States like Amazon, eBay, and BestBuy.com. Nevertheless, price isn't the only consideration for Mexicans. Load time of a site, speed of delivery, customer service, and reliability also are important. So the usability and aesthetics of a site play a part in the purchase decision process as well.

"Right now, we are focused on securing our local markets and ensuring a good buying experience for Mexican shoppers," said Ceballos. "If you want to buy a cell phone in Mexico, you have several alternatives. You can go to a department store. You can go to MercadoLibre. Or you can go to Best Buy, Amazon, or eBay in the United States. So, let's say this buyer ends up buying the phone on Best Buy's U.S. Hispanic site and has a good experience. That's not good for us. Because of that, we focus on creating the best buying experience possible."

Years ago, MercadoLibre had a U.S. site, but company officials closed it as they found that everyone shopped on eBay, probably because most Hispanics at the time were bilingual and e-commerce was in its infancy. Today, 657,000 U.S. Hispanics visit MercadoLibre (ComScore, September 2009). While that only represents only 2.2 percent of its global unique visitors, hundreds of thousands of Spanish speakers are clearly looking for a way to buy products online—and not finding anything. In addition to wire transfers, MercadoLibre accepts international credit cards via its payment solution MercadoPago, similar to PayPal, but U.S. visitors typically do not buy products from Mexico because of the prohibitive shipping costs.

Ceballos admits that MercadoLibre has not found a good way of measuring demand from the United States for purchases in Mexico or vice versa, even though Mexican-Americans may want to buy gifts for their family and friends back home. "There is demand for U.S. Hispanics buying into MercadoLibre Mexico, and there would probably be demand for MercadoLibre to have a U.S. Hispanic site, but then again a lot of the traffic would probably come from Latin America."

ComScore (September 2009) reports that MercadoLibre saw 27 million unique visitors in all of Latin America (including Brazil), representing 91 percent of its traffic, and 1.9 million from Spain, or 6.4 percent of its visitors, where it does not currently do any business. In comparison, eBay.es (from Spain) saw 3.4 million unique users from Spain, or 78 percent of its audience; 894,000 unique users from Latin America, or 20 percent of its audience; and only 96,000 unique users from the United States (ComScore, September 2009). Companies that have Spanish-language sites like VictoriasSecret.com and BestBuy.com saw 218,000 and 453,000 unique visitors, respectively, to their sites in Latin America (Com-Score, September 2009).

Some Surprising Facts about Mexico

About 45 million people live in Spain. In comparison, about 46 million out of 106 million Mexicans (World Bank, World Development Indicators) are middle to upper class, larger than the entire population of Spain. Move over conquistadors, here come the Mexicans.

- The richest man in the world—Carlos Slim Helu—lives in Mexico City with $53.5 billion in assets. (Forbes)
- 80% of Mexican households owned a cell phone in 2009, according to AMIPCI, Mexico's e-commerce association.
- Remittances to Mexico reached US$25.1 billion in 2008 (Banco de Mexico), the second-largest source of foreign income after oil exports.

To further understand the issue of e-commerce in Mexico, let's take a look at MercadoLibre's 2009 annual report. In diving into the numbers, I discovered something surprising about its financial results that validates the numbers in "The International Shopping Traveler Study." In 2009, $54 million of its revenues from sales came from Brazil, $26 million from Venezuela, $23 million from Argentina, $13 million from Mexico, and $10 million from Chile, Colombia, Costa Rica, Dominican Republic, Ecuador, Panama, Peru and Uruguay combined. Plus, it saw $44 million in revenues from its payments business, MercadoPago.

Mexico appears behind Venezuela and Argentina even though Mexico's GDP overshadows both of those countries' GDPs combined. This indicates that Mexicans may shop so much in the United States or on U.S. sites (with better usability like BestBuy.com or Amazon.com) that it negatively affects MercadoLibre Mexico, putting it at number four on the company's list of revenue-generating countries. In addition, it may indicate that Mexico's e-commerce industry is in an earlier state of its infancy relative to other emerging markets. This is an example of one of the great challenges for Latin America and really all emerging markets: very little reliable research exists about consumer behavior online or offline.

In total, MercadoLibre showed revenue of $173 million in 2009, an increase of 26 percent over 2008's $137 million, and it saw 30 million visitors (ComScore, September 2009). This pales in comparison to eBay's $2.3 billion in revenue and 81 million global monthly unique visitors (2008 annual report). As eBay's growth starts to slow and as e-commerce sales adoption plateaus, investors will want to find markets that are three to five years behind our more mature market and invest in growth markets like Latin America.

Lessons Learned

- Consumers always find the best prices for the same product online and even go so far as to plan a trip to the country next door to buy them.
- Mexicans outspend their rivals from Japan, Germany, the UK, and Canada on shopping trips to the United States.
- North American, Spanish-language websites by default target U.S. Hispanics *and* the middle- and upper-class Mexicans who use the web.
- Consider building dedicated websites for international shoppers as Macy's did with its VisitMacysUSA.com website.
- Word travels quickly about well-designed, fast websites with good selection and low prices, especially since they typically are better optimized for search.
- User-generated content, reviews, and services are by their nature global.
- The majority of Mexican shoppers visiting the United States are below the age of 40, part of Mexico's baby boom.
- Mexico's middle and upper class is larger than the entire population of Spain.

U.S. Hispanics: A Proxy for Understanding the Mexican e-Commerce Market

**By Roxana Strohmenger
and Tamara Barber
Forrester Research, Inc.**

Why is it that U.S. Hispanic and Mexican consumers—in two markets that are geographically close and culturally similar—show such uniquely distinct e-commerce behaviors? In the U.S., the Hispanic e-commerce market is strong with 88 percent of online adult buyers purchasing a product or service online during Q3 of 2009.[1] In stark contrast, the Mexican e-commerce market is in its infancy with only 14 percent of online adult buyers purchasing online. While there are many key factors affecting the size of the e-commerce market in Mexico, such as concerns regarding Internet security and reliability of shipping products to the customer, our focus here is to highlight the online consumer's overall experience with the Internet as a critical factor in e-commerce adoption. For retailers to effectively build strategies to grow the Mexican e-commerce market, we suggest that you can use as a lens the growth and characteristics of the Hispanic e-commerce market over the past several years. To provide some context, let's examine the lives of two average adult buyers who have purchased a product or service online during Q3 of 2009—Roberto, from Mexico, and Esteban, from the U.S.

Roberto is a 30-year old Mexican online buyer who, like most Mexican online adults, has been using the Internet for about 5 years (see graphic at right). However, he actually spends more time web surfing each week (15 hours) than the rest of his online peers (10 hours). He sees the advantages of technology and embraces the possibilities. Given his focus on career, he is benefiting from a larger amount of discretionary funds compared with Mexican online adults overall. Esteban, on the other hand, is an older online buyer at 35 years of age, and is a U.S.-born Hispanic.[2] His online tenure and average weekly time surfing the web is equal to that of Hispanic online adults as a whole. Like Roberto, he is optimistic about technology. At this point in his life, his career is still important, but other motivations like family are becoming a priority. Esteban's discretionary funds are slightly larger than his online peers but not to the same degree as Roberto's.

The differences in the lives of these two average online adult buyers cannot be boiled down to access, since Internet adoption is the same for both groups—52 percent for U.S. Hispanic adults and 53 percent for Mexican adults.[3] However, tenure—and thus experience online—plays a key role in the development of an e-commerce audience. Roberto has been online for less than half the time of Esteban. He is still learning about the concepts of e-commerce and has concerns over whether it is safe and if he will get exactly what he purchased when it shows up at his front door. Roberto is also still trying to understand the advantage of ordering online versus just getting into the car and driving to the store.

Online tenure and usage differ significantly between Mexican and US Hispanic online adults

	Mexican Online Adults	Roberto: A Mexican Online Buyer*	US Hispanic Online Adults	Esteban: US Hispanic Online Buyer*
Male	55%	66%	54%	57%
Mean age	31	30	35	35
Mean household income (Mexico: monthly; US: annual)	$837†	$1,181†	$57,300	$69,210
Online buyer (*past 3 months*)	14%	100%	88%	100%
Mean offline spend (past 3 months)	$347†	$617†	$627	$563
Mean online spend (*past 3 months*)	$43†	$329†	$298	$348
Technology optimist	62%	72%	62%	65%
Career motivated	34%	42%	28%	29%
Mean online tenure (years)	4	5	11	11
Mean hours online (per week)	10	15	23	24

Base: 1,656 Mexican online adults; 213 Mexican online buyers; 2,886 US Hispanic online adults; 2,474 US Hispanic online buyers.

* Online buyers are online adults who have purchased a product or service online in the past 3 months.

† For comparative purposes, the monetary amounts for Mexico were converted using the following conversion rate as of April 2010 (MXN 1 = .0818351 USD).

Source: Latin American Technographics® Benchmark Survey, Q3 2009 (Mexico, Brazil); Hispanic Technographics® Adult Online Survey, Q3 2009 (US)

When trying to carve a slice out of the Mexican e-commerce market, retailers need to create an experience that will minimize the hesitations of consumers like Roberto and more importantly his online peers who are not yet purchasing online. And these experiences need to be proven over time. For example, three years ago there were four main roadblocks to Hispanics' online shopping in the U.S.:

- 48% of online Hispanics did not want to give out personal financial information;
- 46% wanted to be able to see things before buying;
- 26% had heard about bad experiences purchasing online; and
- 23% did not have access to a credit card or debit card (see graphic below).

Three years later, in 2009, these statistics had decreased to 22%, 39%, 11% and 9% respectively.

Over time, US Hispanic online adults have become more comfortable purchasing online

"Why haven't you bought or ordered products or services online in the past 3 months?"

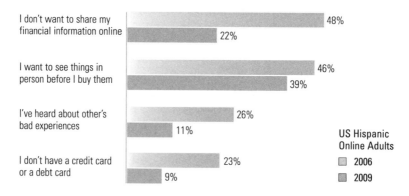

Base: 719 US Hispanic online adults who have not purchased online in the past 3 months in 2008 (multiple responses accepted). 659 US Hispanic online adults who have not purchased online in the past 3 months in 2009 (multiple responses accepted).

Source: Hispanic American Technology Adoption Survey, Spring 2006 Online Survey; Hispanic Technographics® Adult Online Survey, Q3 2009 (US)

Using this as a proxy for how e-commerce markets develop, Mexican retailers should consider how to quell these specific concerns. Consider steps such as: developing relationships with companies like Verisign, creating interactive tools to help customers get a feel for the product, making the purchase process smooth and efficient in conjunction with good customer service, and providing multiple payment methods.

Retailers should also keep in mind, though, that both the Robertos and Estebans of the world still use the Internet to research products online and purchase them offline (48% and 47% respectively for Mexican and U.S. Hispanic online buyers). In both these markets, retailers need to explore making the cross-channel experience seamless. For example, Walmart offers a service called "Site to Store®" where customers can order online and pick up items in the store, and Benjamin Moore has an online product demonstration tool called "Personal Color Viewer®" for previewing how a specific paint will look in a room.

The Internet, for both Roberto and Esteban, is now one tool that they use to help educate themselves and make decisions within and across channels. The rate at which the e-commerce market grows in Mexico will be tied to how well retailers embrace the online needs and offline retail behaviors of consumers like Roberto. As experience tells us with U.S. Hispanics, online consumers need to feel they have a secure, simple, and interactive experience in order to make online shopping more mainstream.

Notes

1. An online adult buyer is defined as an individual who goes on the internet at least once a month or more and has purchased a product or service in the past 3 months (irrespective of channel). In addition, note that while the data presented compares online Mexican consumers to online US Hispanic consumers, the survey methodology used to collect this data was different. The Mexican data comes from face-to-face interviews using a multistage stratified random sample methodology. In contrast the US Hispanic data, except where noted, comes from an online survey where we drew a random sample of respondents from a managed access panel of online consumers. Finally, note that the Mexican data is only representative of the top 10 markets in Mexico (specifically: México City, Guadalajara, Monterrey, Puebla, Toluca, Tijuana, León, Juárez, Veracruz, and Mérida).

2. Specifically, Forrester found that 65% of US Hispanic online adults and 64% of US Hispanic online buyers (like Roberto) are US-born.

3. The US Hispanic data comes from Forrester's Technographics® Media and Marketing Phone Survey, Q1 2009 (US). Note that the date was collected using a random digit dial (RDD) methodology with two subsamples: one random sample using RDD and one using RDD within geographic areas that are at least 33% Hispanic according to the 2000 US Census.

Chapter 5

Lessons in Social Media

WHEN Christopher Columbus landed in the Bahamas in October 1492, he called the natives "Indians" thinking that he was actually in the Orient. He continued exploring, making two subsequent voyages to these newfound territories, wondering whether he had indeed landed in Asia. Geographers and explorers disputed his claim, thinking that this was a completely "new world." Sadly, instead of embracing his "discovery," Columbus died a wealthy but disappointed and defeated man, having not discovered what he truly wanted, the riches of the Orient.

The story of Fotolog, a photo-sharing and social networking site, highlights how history can repeat itself, but with a different result. The site originally set out to offer its service to Americans, specifically in Brooklyn, and landed on a completely different geographic location. Instead of rejecting what it had discovered, the company made the best of its "new world." It is important to consider the ramifications of this lesson for marketers like Lexicon Marketing (whose case study was featured in chapter 1) who have incorporated social networking as a key strategy for engaging Hispanics online.

What If Your Customers Take You to Latin America?

In 2002, Scott Heiferman, now famous for starting MeetUp.com, and Adam Seifer launched Fotolog as an online community for their friends in Brooklyn to post photos and share them. Instead of building up a domestic fan base, as they thought would happen, their user base took them down an unexpected path, according to Yossi Langer, chief product officer, and Arne "Joe" Jokela, chief technology officer of Fotolog.

In 2005, Heiferman and Seifer's friend, Cora Ronai, a journalist from Brazil, visited New York and was impressed by their site. She returned home, wrote an article about Fotolog for O Globo, Brazil's leading newspaper, and within two months, Brazilian users outnumbered American users. The popularity of Fotolog spread to Argentina and Chile in 2006 and then jumped the Atlantic Ocean to Spain and Portugal in 2007. That same year, traffic took off in the North of Mexico, especially around Monterrey. In 2010, Spain became their number one country, in terms of users.

Because the site hosts user-generated content and photos, it became a Portuguese- and Spanish-language site seemingly overnight. U.S. visitors now represent less than 5 percent of its total traffic, and the site officially offers 12 languages. According to ComScore (September 2009), Fotolog saw 9.8 million visitors across Latin America, 2.4 million visitors in Spain, and only 389,000 in the United States. Alexa (June 2010) shows Fotolog as the 15th most popular site in Argentina and 11th most popular site in Chile.

In an article on the BBC Mundo, David Cuen wrote (in Spanish), "According to Insites Consulting, Latin America has the highest usage of social networks in percentage terms. And in accordance with these statistics, 95 percent of Latin American Internet users have one account in at least one social network, an important growth rate if we consider that only one year ago eMarketer reported that 87 percent of Latin Americans online used social networks." (March 24, 2010)

Why is Fotolog still based in New York if only 5 percent of its user base lives in the United States? Langer and Jokela say that New York affords them connections to the investment, media, and technology communities and a global perspective from which they can put together deals as needed. If they were to move their corporate headquarters to the city where they had the greatest number of users at any one time, in early

2009 it would have been Madrid; in the summer of 2009 it would have been Buenos Aires; and in early 2010 it would have been Santiago, Chile. Fotolog's holding company, Hi-Media, based in Paris, has three main business units: an online advertising network, a content network, including Fotolog, where users pay for premium subscriptions, and mobile payments services, the fastest-growing area of its business

Advertising was Fotolog's main source of revenue until Hi-Media launched its mobile payment product, at which point the premium content subscriptions took off. Why? Not many young Latin Americans have credit cards. The mobile payment service enabled Fotolog users to charge their premium subscriptions to their cell phone bills.

Langer, Jokela, and Fotolog's marketing team regularly converse with their users by email, sometimes even meeting with them in person. One "flogger" (short for photo blogger on Fotolog) in particular caught their attention. Agustina Vivero, who goes by the username "Cumbio," started using the site when she was 14 and says that Fotolog provided a good platform for figuring out her identity. ("Cumbio" is a play on the word "Cumbia," a tropical-sounding dance music popular in Argentina, Colombia, and the Caribbean.) In contrast, she said Facebook felt like putting yourself in a box. She uses Fotolog to connect with friends and organize weekly get-togethers at the Abasto shopping mall in Buenos Aires. The Sunday night events have become so popular that they have spilled over to other nights of the week. Argentinean teenagers gather to socialize, but, in addition, Cumbio invites educational speakers to the events to inform her followers about sexual health.

LatinoLink

Fotolog.com/Cumbio

Cumbio became Argentina's first Internet celebrity. Nike asked her to endorse its 3DG customizable shoes, the makers of Big Brother approached her with a reality TV show series, and a local political party asked her to run for office. She accepted the deal with Nike, but the reality TV show did not work out, and she has opted to finish school instead of running for office. At left is the promo for her book.

Here is an excerpt from a *New York Times* article ("In Argentina, a Camera and a Blog Make a Star," March 13, 2009) about Cumbio:

The Cumbio craze really took off after Guillermo Tragant, president of Furia, a marketing company, discovered Ms. Vivero and the floggers last April [2008] while scouting for fresh faces for a Nike sportswear campaign. Nike wanted "real people from the streets," Mr. Tragant said. "The power of the image for them is so strong," he said, noting the afternoon "matinee" parties where floggers gather and walk a catwalk posing for photos of one another. "The sensation that the famous floggers are living today is like what Hollywood movie stars experience walking the red carpet."

To use Malcolm Gladwell's term from *The Tipping Point*, we can call Cumbio a "connector," or someone who brings together many people who share a common interest. Clearly, she has great influence over her followers on Fotolog, as the hundreds of mall-goers have turned into thousands, and she has written a best-selling autobiography telling the story of her rise to fame (without even having finished high school). She makes more money for a brief nightclub appearance than her father, a plumber, earns in two days.

So what does Cumbio have to do with your company? As Nike has shown, the "connectors" in a society can be a great asset. Your brand may be able to identify influencers among your target Latino audience online, as Nike has with Cumbio. What social networks do they use? What do they discuss online? What events do they organize and attend offline?

Originally, Fotolog found that about 80 percent of its users knew everyone on their "friends" list. The results of a survey in January 2010, seems to show that has changed. Langer says, "People have become more promiscuous about adding users as friends. Now, 18 percent of users say they know everyone on their list while 51 percent of them know more than half of users on the list." So, most people on Fotolog know only half of the people on their contacts list.

This actually represents good news for companies that want to exponentially add contacts to their Facebook, Twitter, or other social networking pages. Your company can reach a vast array of users through a single influential flogger, like Cumbio, to build your audience. Then, once recommended, Fotolog's survey indicates that you can add followers that you don't know personally, but that find your content helpful and useful.

Two Types of "Connectors" Online

"Generally, on Fotolog, there are two kinds of 'popular' accounts: hubs and connectors," according to Danielle Goldstein, a longtime community associate at Fotolog. "'Hubs' are the 'superstars,' whose fame is somewhat superficial. They're the ones people want to be associated with and the ones that people will sign up for an account to keep up with, but they probably won't do much with the account otherwise. It's a one-way interest; the 'superstar' really only cares about the fans as far as they make them popular. And the fans don't really care about each other," Goldstein says.

In contrast, "connectors" are the ones that rise more slowly; they're usually longtime members, and if they don't work or function in a social group of a kind, then they're at least found on the follower list of everyone interested in that particular area or theme. These people encourage "fans" and followers to communicate, to follow each other by providing a common fandom/space that everyone can participate in. Everyone typically knows one another in a connector's circle.

Most members are a mix of these two types Goldstein finds, and users react to these two types of members differently.

"Cumbio started as a connector in a local sense and slowly turned into a hub as the number of her 'fans' increased to an unmanageable level," says Goldstein. "With regards to the reactions to these two types of users, hubs are generally polarizing: either you are a fan or you don't like them. Connectors, on the other hand, foster a community around a shared common interest and only see adverse reactions to the area of interest they focus on but are not attacked personally."

Finding people on social networks with a lot of contacts is easy. But finding a "connector" that has actually made real, substantial connections online and offline, as Nike discovered in Cumbio, can be quite difficult. You can use a system through which you filter out "hubs" to find the real "connectors" as exemplified in the diagram below. You start by measuring the number of contacts they have. Then you analyze the quality of their connections and content through the number and regularity of the comments on the connector's page. Last, find out where connectors attend offline events to see how many people show up, as Cumbio did at the Abasto shopping mall.

Bringing Music Fans Together on YouTube and MySpace

Larry Hernandez wears a cowboy hat when he sings his brand of Northern Mexican Ranchera music. He uploads videos to his YouTube channel from his concerts or his daily, personal life when he walks around the towns he visits, doing something funny. In this manner, he constantly keeps in touch with his audience. Fans return to his YouTube channel often to watch his videos and especially when he posts exclusive content. Erika Nuño, the Director of Latin marketing for Universal Music Group, says that Larry is a perfect example of how to manage a personal brand online via social networks.

Word-of-mouth marketing serves as his primary tactic in getting his message out about these videos and extending his fan base beyond Mexico. On top of announcing and promoting his website and his MySpace page at all of his shows, Larry tells his fans that they may be included in the upcoming videos. That encourages his fans to log onto his YouTube channel to view the videos and thus, the buzz spreads about his online activity and his visibility grows. Most importantly, by building an online audience in Northern Mexico (where he is from), his fans spread the word about his music online by sharing his YouTube and MySpace pages with friends and family in the U.S., thus enabling him to grow a fan base across the border in the U.S. and even other countries in Latin America.

> **LatinoLink**
>
> YouTube.com/malandrodepu
> MySpace.com/LarryHernandez

Artists who constantly post content online and promote themselves actively during their live performances significantly increase their opportunities to reach more individuals and build a larger fan base. When artists themselves manage their presence on social networks and personally connect with their fans, it not only keeps the pages active and updated but also builds a more loyal audience.

Building Your Brand on Facebook

"To seduce almost anyone, ask for and listen to his opinion," said Malcolm Forbes. Perhaps if Steve Forbes would have followed his dad's advice and asked Internet users "What's on your mind?" as Facebook asks its users, he could have grown his audience to nearly 500 million unique visitors around the world as Mark Zuckerberg, the founder of Facebook, has.

Now, the question becomes, how can Facebook make lasting impressions between its advertisers and members. In order to generate new demand for products, marketers need to move up the consumer funnel, says Blake Chandlee, Facebook's vice president of sales for Latin America, Eastern Europe, and Asia. "The power of the social graph is changing the discovery process. The network of real connections through which people communicate and share information is the most influential way to reach someone." More specifically, marketers can tap into these networks by using a variety of targeting methods with information from Facebook users' profiles like age, gender, interests, and marital status.

How can brands grow their fan base in a specific countries or regions? Chandlee says, "In many cases today brands, celebrities, politicians, television shows, local restaurants and businesses will most likely build a page on Facebook where they establish a community. The advantage is that activity that takes place here has organic and viral attributes that allow brands to expand their presence through friends and families of their fans. By having the ability to publish into the newsfeeds of their fans, and delivering a message or content that is compelling enough for their fans to share, the brands can become part of the social fabric of people's lives. This requires a commitment from brands to have an ongoing relationship and dialogue with users, to be authentic, to bring value to users consistent with their expectations, and to listen as much as publish. Brands such as Starbucks, Adidas, Nike, Ben & Jerry's, AXE and others benefit from building robust, active and thriving communities."

A Formula for Developing Content Communities

Gumersindo Lafuente created an innovative community content portal that blended community, technology, and editorial when he founded SoiTu.es. Today, he runs the editorial team for ElPais.com, one of the largest Spanish-language news sites in the world. Media companies and marketers alike can follow his innovations for fostering content communities online

First, Lafuente aimed to figure out new ways to distribute and better integrate community, technology, and news editorial. Most media companies organizations, he feels, focus far too much on the editorial. This is why he hired programmers to work in-house, sit next to the editorial team, and develop all of SoiTu's own back-end systems, most notably its own proprietary micro-blogging service for journalists that scanned text, suggested tags, and created a better way to organize journalistic information. Readers appreciated the many ways to find helpful information including search tools by keyword, theme, date, and fully integrated social media–style commenting, encouraging users to register on the site.

Second, SoiTu cultivated its core community of journalists and editors by inviting its most loyal readers and fans to share news in its service called "El Selector de Noticias," or "The Selector of News," a community-powered feed where SoiTu users could recommend articles from third-party sites. By enabling readers to share what they thought was most interest-

ing or relevant to the community members, SoiTu built confidence in its own branded community, encouraging them to return to SoiTu again and again.

Third, SoiTu's "I♥Publi," or "I love advertising," blog brought together outside experts on advertising, design, and media with its advertising team to cover trends in marketing communications. This channel integrated advertising into the community-oriented content, creating conversation between reader and advertiser, instead of dividing editorial and advertising teams as often happens within media companies.

Last, SoiTu.es cultivated relationships with its community of "prosumer" reader-contributor-promoters. These contributors developed content, shared it with friends, and invited even more new reader-writers and fans. For example, SoiTu invited the illustrator Gabi Campanario, a native of Barcelona, to write for its Urban Life channel about the goings-on in his current hometown of Seattle. He scanned drawings from his notebook documenting daily life, and explained them in accompanying blog posts. He built such a following of fellow illustrators on SoiTu, that he eventually broke off to start his own community site of illustrators who wanted to share scans of their notebook illustrations.

More than 150 writers from around the Spanish-speaking world, like Gabi Campanario, contributed to SoiTu—most of whom were unpaid—about subjects that deeply interested them such as movies, music, trends, digital life, health, food, gastronomy, design, and architecture. Writers, architects, designers, advertising professionals, students, and professors pitched their stories to the editorial staff, who would then approve and edit the stories.

A few marketers have successfully blended community, technology, and editorial, like the Nike+ site, which measures and analyzes a runner's workouts, connects runners to other runners, and enables runners to share their favorite running routes. This exemplifies how a marketer can successfully become a publisher by using the community + technology + editorial formula.

The big challenge in building communities online is how audiences spill across borders globally and then selling the ad space to support those communities in markets like Latin America where CPM's can cost four times less than in the U.S. Or, on community-driven product review sites, the challenge becomes driving shoppers to their local, country-specific e-commerce sites, accepting international credit cards, and ensuring delivery.

According to ComScore, as many as 49 percent (November 2008) and as few as 22 percent (September 2009) of SoiTu's visitors came from Latin America. Interestingly, Lafuente noticed that, when SoiTu launched an editorial product or community for Mexico, *without any advertising, promotion, or even an email to contacts there,* the traffic there would immediately spike.

While most companies do not advertise globally, the movie industry launches films globally on the same day in order to avoid problems with piracy. Warner Bros., Universal, and the other film studios now develop global advertising and marketing programs to fight this issue. In the future, virtual products like music, travel reservations, and now books (with the Kindle and other electronic readers) must consider global sales strategies and advertising plans because of demand across the web.

Because of the explosive growth of online communities and the emotional power of word-of-mouth recommendations made on social networks, marketers may want to consider developing global or pan-regional advertising and communications programs by language to better meet the needs of consumers who influence one another on sites like SoiTu or Facebook.

Beta-Testing Communities and Content

Massimo Martinotti, the founder of the boutique production agency, Mia Films in Miami oftentimes beta-tests niche content ideas on his video blog, Facebook, and Twitter to see what does and doesn't resonate with consumers in online communities. He does this in preparation for developing content ideas for his clients like Sony, Toyota, Kellogg's, and Corona. For example, he launched a number of talk show format videos where a host and an expert discuss the *"tecnicas del beso,"* or the techniques of a good kiss. Within months, the community grew to over 30,000 users and today the content has become self-sustaining where users contribute subdued (not risqué) photos and videos of couples kissing. Both women and men participate and the community sure would lend itself to a marketing campaign for Dentyne or Wrigley's.

Once he develops niche content ideas, he strives to tell synergic stories for marketers that cannot squeeze into a single medium but rather evolve across multiple platforms in which converging stories can live and grow. "The user's experience unfolds across as many media as possible and every single platform makes idiosyncratic and distinctive contributions to the story," says Martinotti. "A story will possibly start with a short webisode. However, for users to understand it, they will eventually have to follow the characters of the story on Twitter, join a group on Facebook or Flickr, visit a channel on YouTube or Vimeo, receive or send SMS texts or MMS, participate in a forum or a chat, play a game or an alternate reality game, attend an event, and so forth."

Ten-Step Process to Managing Social Media

Of all of the self-proclaimed "social media experts," Sally Falkow of Pro-active Report, based in Pasadena, California, brings seriousness to the social media PR business with her 10-step process to working with social media:

1. **Listen:** What is your target audience discussing online? What suggestions or complaints do they share about your company, your products, or your competition?

2. **Share of voice:** What percentage of the conversations does your company participate in for your product line, target audience, or geographic region?

3. **Set goals and benchmarks:** What do you want to accomplish in social media and once you launch an initiative what are the benchmarks to measure success?

4. **Find communities and bloggers that matter:** Who are the thought

leaders you want to connect to? What communities focus on your industry or discuss your products?

5. **Identify influencers:** Who are the Cumbios and how can you leverage them as Nike did?

6. **Create a content strategy:** What information will users find helpful that build trust with your audience? What scope of ideas should be considered and how can you focus on the most useful or relevant areas of content?

7. **Choose tools:** These might include content management systems, social media platforms, distribution (RSS feeds), search technologies, and sharing tools.

8. **Create and deliver content:** Who can you partner with to develop content?

9. **Engage in and facilitate conversations:** How can social media translate into a proactive customer service channel? Can this translate into a greater, more profitable lifetime value between your customers and your company?

10. **Measure:** What ROI metrics do you want to use to measure success? Retweeted content? Links to your site? New emails registered? Complaints received and fixed? New business ideas received?

Building Communities via Promotions on Blogs

In June 2009, the Cervantes Institute of Chicago launched a short story contest on its blog with the goal of engaging local writers and Spanish students in the Chicago area. What happened provides a perfect example of how expectations of launching a Spanish-language promotion or website do not conform to the borderless reality of the worldwide web. Salvador Vergara, of the Cervantes Institute Chicago, told me that they never expected entrants from outside of the United States. Instead, they were shocked to find that more than 70 percent of their entrants were not only from outside of the Chicago area but also from outside of the United States entirely. They received entries from countries such as Argentina, Brazil, Holland, Venezuela, Spain, and even the Ukraine. Many Hispanic marketing managers who launch promotions online find similar experiences at their companies.

Modeled after programs like Germany's Goethe Institute and France's Alliance Française, the government of Spain created the Instituto Cervantes in 1991 to promote the study of the Spanish language and culture at 54 centers in 20 countries, with facilities in New York, Chicago, Rio de Janeiro, Tokyo, London, and Beijing, among others. Named after Miguel de Cervantes (1547–1616), the author of *Don Quixote* and arguably the most important figure in Spanish literature, the Cervantes Institute has established itself as a leading resource for Spanish language and culture globally. It makes sense, then, that the contest would attract Spanish speakers worldwide who share a passion for creative writing, because participants see themselves as participating in a prestigious brand. The Cervantes Institute took advantage of this unexpected windfall of visitors and published an e-book of the short story winners online, making its blog the hub of Spanish-language writers.

The Cervantes Institute successfully tapped into a community of writers passionate about a common theme—short stories—and encouraged them to submit their own work. It did several things right in managing its local marketing initiative. The institute successfully used new technologies to highlight its editorial content including WordPress for its blog; SnapShots as a preview tool; and Issuu, a digital publishing platform for showcasing the winners of the short story contest as a virtual book.

From August to December 2009, the Cervantes Institute's Chicago blog saw visitors from the following countries:

Country	Percentage
Spain	38.6%
United States	18.5%
Argentina	13%
Mexico	10.8%
Colombia	5.8%
Chile	4%
Venezuela	3%
Peru	3%

Source: ClustrMaps tool on the Cervantes Institute's Chicago blog, August 2009 to December 2009

In hindsight, The Cervantes Institute could have improved the contest or more clearly delineated who the contest was for by explaining in its rules that the contest was for "citizens of the state of Illinois." Larger publishers and marketers can provide a welcome mat to their visitors from foreign IPs with landing pages saying, "Thanks for coming, but this contest is only available for people in the USA." While that filters out foreigners, you may risk coming across as overly exclusive or filtering out Americans living abroad, for example. Alternatively, you could ask foreigners coming to your site a few questions to understand how they found your site and why they came.

A marketing manager at Burger King told me that they find the same issue as Instituto Cervantes found. Its online contests and sweepstakes for U.S. Hispanics (in Spanish) are meant to target U.S. citizens, yet many Mexicans, Argentineans, and even Spaniards find the sites and enter online, mostly due to the search trends discussed in Chapter 2. The reverse is also true. When Burger King runs a promotion in Mexico, it receives entrants from U.S. Hispanics and Spain. Nevertheless, Burger King targets its online advertising for U.S. Hispanics in the United States to focus its marketing efforts on its intended market.

The Cervantes Institute turned its unexpected visitors into an opportunity by publishing its e-book. Any global brand like Burger King or the Cervantes Institute will most likely experience this challenge since their brands have locations across the Spanish-language world. Instead of randomly finding users from around the world on your website, use the localization and globalization techniques outlined in Chapter 8 to ensure that your brand funnels these users to the correct international website.

Lessons Learned

- Social networking sites that grow globally, on the upside, reflect the idea that users around the world can universally appreciate a site's design and functionality. On the downside, users from outside of a social network's home country can "take over" a site if they find the site to be useful.

- Influential "connectors" can help marketers reach and persuade teenagers or other consumers, as Cumbio did for Nike. Online social networks make finding "connectors" easier than ever.

- It is important to consider the ramifications of the global nature of social media for marketers like Lexicon Marketing (featured in chapter 1) who have developed their own branded social network as a key strategy for engaging Hispanics online.

- Popular social media profiles can be categorized into either "hubs" or "connectors." "Hubs" are superstars that everyone adds as a follower with typically superficial fame. "Connectors" can be found on the follower list of everyone interested in a particular area or theme, which encourage followers to communicate with one other by providing a common space that everyone can participate in.

- Forums or discussion groups are by their nature global.

  – Develop local voices by integrating bloggers into editorial offerings.

  – New combinations of community, technology, and editorial will foster the new wave of innovation in online publishing.

  – Invite your active readers to become contributors to your website, as we saw with the story of the illustrator, Gabi Campanario, on SoiTu

  – Establish and use a process for working with social media sites including steps like listening, analyzing share of your brand's voice, setting goals and benchmarks, identifying influencers and connectors, creating content development and delivery strategies, choosing web tools, and measuring results.

Why U.S. Hispanics Use Social Networking Sites

By Felipe Korzenny, Ph.D.,
Professor and Director
Center for Hispanic Marketing Communication,
Florida State University

In 2009, The Florida State University Center for Hispanic Marketing Communication and DMS Research in collaboration with Captura Group collected online national level data about Hispanics' use of social networking sites. The main motivation of this study was to find out what reasons, attitudes, preferences, and demographics contribute to the time Hispanics spend on social networking sites online. The national online Hispanic sub-sample was composed of almost 541 Hispanics who answered the questionnaire in English and 351 who answered in Spanish.

LatinoLink

HMC.comm.fsu.edu

The dependent variable of this study—that is, the behavior we were attempting to explain—is the number of hours that Hispanics/Latinos reported spending while "visiting social networking sites on an average week." This specific study included a mix of 80 general attitudes, preferences, and reasons and behaviors relevant to online activities and participation in social networking sites.

We observed that, in general, the more time Latinos spend using the Internet, be it in Spanish or English, the more time they spend on social networking sites. Thus, online familiarity and activity appear to create a propensity for participation in social media online. The key reasons why Hispanics spend time on social networking sites is for messaging, blogging, self-expression, making new friends, and sharing cherished images. The reasons that were least important for using social networking sites included promoting my business, promoting causes, asking questions, answering questions, commenting on people's activities, telling stories, chatting, and using classifieds. That messaging and overall self-expression constitute central reasons for Latinos to connect online makes sense. In this and other research, we have found that self-expression is one of the strong motivators of Hispanics generally. Thus, the Internet has become a most important liberating technology that allows repressed social needs to be expressed. Hispanics, in particular, are fond of sharing their experiences.

Other factors strongly associated with time spent on visiting social networking sites included reading magazines in English, being younger, and being concerned about one's diet. That younger Latinos spend more time on social networking sites is not surprising. What is surprising is that, while age is important, it is not nearly as important as other factors and reasons as more older Hispanics get turned on to social networks online. Reading magazines in English seems to imply that the type of people who are on social networks tend to be generally "print or text" oriented and curious about the world around them. Interestingly, concern about one's diet may be partially addressed by social networks where Hispanics share issues and information of importance. Perhaps those who are more socially active are also more concerned about their health and appearance, and hence their diet is very important to them. Accordingly, food and fitness advertisers are likely to benefit from being more active and visible in social networks where Latinos share their experiences. Notably, gender was not found to make a difference in this analysis.

Marketers and service providers can capitalize on research like this by understanding that, by facilitating messaging and self-expression online, they are likely to attract the interest of Latinos. There are few reasons that are most important for attracting Hispanics to social networks online, and this research should serve as a step in that direction. Advertisers should consider embedding and linking to social networks where Hispanics participate to facilitate interaction and self-expression. Merchant websites should also consider the importance that Latinos assign to self-expression and sociability and facilitate these activities on their sites. As a corollary, I should emphasize that it seems like the age of corporate and organizational censoring is being replaced by an age of openness.

Chapter 6

Organize Your Team and Align Its Goals

"IF EVERYONE is moving forward together, then success takes care of itself," Henry Ford said. That is precisely what this chapter addresses: how to organize your teams to best meet the needs of the Hispanic and Latin American markets where you do business.

Maintain a Single, Central Web Platform

One of the most important lessons in organizing successful web initiatives for multiple brands, countries, or ethnic targets is to integrate your assets into one central unit. For years, global e-commerce players like Amazon and eBay have managed their technology platforms centrally, which enables them to roll out new sites across the world. You need to leverage your content management, database, product catalog software and CRM technology investment across markets. For example, Yahoo! merged its North and South American regions, including U.S. Hispanic, to form the "Americas" region, which allows the company to manage content relationships, search development, ad sales, and other areas to foster growth in Latin America and Brazil. BabyCenter manages its editorial in San Francisco and then localizes its editorial with a team based in each market where it expands.

Another lesson here is not to isolate U.S. Hispanic online initiatives (English and Spanish) on separate websites; instead, integrate them into one content management system and user experience so that bilingual users can easily switch between the sites. Certain types of sites such as portals and informational sites lend themselves to a centralized system easier than others. Your website increasingly provides the first contact that many potential customers have with your brand(s). The navigation should allow visitors to switch between languages and countries. It should be helpful, friendly, and appealing with the aim of beginning a relationship that provides helpful products and services to the consumer yet profitable lifetime value for the marketer.

In January 2010, Walmart followed Amazon, eBay, and others in reorganizing its web operations into a single, global e-commerce unit, according to *Internet Retailer*. Walmart calls its central web team site Global.com (not to be confused with Global Automation, Inc., which owns the global.com URL) and gave it the goal of driving sales growth in all of the markets where it has an e-commerce presence online, including the United States, the UK, Canada, Mexico, and Brazil. The company also integrated its Walmart.com U.S. division more closely with its store operations. The unit works to develop global e-commerce strategies and to create a single global e-commerce platform that can be used in every market.

Don DePalma, the founder and chief research officer of Common Sense Advisory, says that by deciding to make e-commerce part of its multi-channel strategy, Walmart made the right choice. Here are three things that he suggests you consider if you have a presence outside of the United States, as Walmart does:

- Develop and execute a global strategy for e-commerce.
- Establish cross-functional and cross-border relationships designed to accelerate and broaden your growth globally online.
- Roll out technology platforms and applications in every market in an effective manner. The global online group can build upon the work of the domestic site, thus enabling the multinational and multicultural teams to leverage the existing investment in technology and process.

In addition, multinationals need to develop cross-market platforms across all of their operations in those markets where they have a physical presence. Walmart can emulate Best Buy's practice of integrated systems that link stores and its website for better customer service. "Where it doesn't have bricks and mortar, it can work with its distribution partners to simplify shipments, returns, and problem resolution with customers. In addition, it can set up multilingual call centers for customer care that meet the needs of both online and in-store customers," says DePalma.

Chuck Whiteman of MotionPoint, a website translation, hosting, and globalization company, also sees his translation and localization clients moving toward centrally managed infrastructures, where they can enjoy massive cost efficiencies with a single digital platform. "By approaching multiple markets and languages correctly, it's possible to save a lot of time and money in the ongoing deployment and management of global websites," he says. In addition, this can provide much tighter brand continuity and timeliness across markets. Whiteman compares it to baking cakes. You can bake 10 different cakes from the same recipe, or websites, and put different frosting on each one while still using the same cake flavor underneath.

Flexible technology platforms allow you to manage your website and translation tools for both the Hispanic and Latin American markets while also incorporating more advanced features that may vary by market such as customer service, community building, specialty content, videos, and product listings of what you sell in each market. Logistical features in the platform may include sales, tax, shipment, and returns data management. "Think about this holistically, and figure out how to reuse or leverage these technologies, processes, and competencies across borders; otherwise, you will build a 'complexity bomb' that will ultimately cost you enormous amounts of money and time to keep it running. Something like this is always a work in progress," says DePalma.

How many localized sites and languages does your company support? If you only manage one or two domestic websites, then it is quite simple. But your strategy will change significantly as you add more sites to your infrastructure. With 20 brand sites in multiple countries or languages, or even multiple domestic markets like the Hispanic and general market, you will need to carefully consider your site architecture and your globalization and localization strategy. "Begin with a visual solution, and build your information architecture from there," says John Yunker, of Byte Level Research.

The following diagram exemplifies what many companies have today:

isolated websites that ought to be integrated, as the second diagram shows. The localization and globalization techniques in Chapter 8 will outline how to steer users to the right websites for each market.

Before: What many companies have today—isolated websites

After: How to connect your international websites under one .com site

Source: Business Without Borders, *Donald A. DePalma, Globa Vista Press, 2002–2004, p. 186, Figure 8.1, Consolidate International Branding Sites. Used with permission.*

Bumeran: Balancing Centralized and Localized Operations

As an example of how to manage country-specific, localized websites across Spanish-language markets while centralizing core functions, you can follow

the lead of Mateo Cuadras, the general manager of Bumeran Venezuela, who previously ran its operations in Mexico. Bumeran is a job search site. Bumeran's country-specific job-search sites are spread across Latin America, and, in some aspects, the sites operate almost as separate companies with different management, job listings, resume databases, sales teams, and client management. Each Bumeran country team adapts its site in the Spanish variant unique to that country.

In contrast, its corporate office in Argentina manages the central marketing, technology, finance, and HR functions. Bumeran takes advantage of its larger scale centrally when negotiating with suppliers. Bumeran also offers global content, across all of its sites, which aims to provide job seekers with tips for improving their job search. Even though some of this content is produced locally (e.g., in Venezuela), it is posted globally across all of the country sites. Bumeran manages its traffic acquisition strategy centrally while directing online users to each country-specific site, for example, the Venezuelan home page or job posting pages.

For other pan-regional brands online, Cuadras recommends that companies take a close look at which functions can be global and which should be localized. This will provide good economies of scale and help your profitability. In addition, he says, "About expanding into new markets, no two countries in Latin America are alike. Maintain local job functions for areas that are only country-specific."

Ways to Effectively Structure Your Organization

Connect Multicultural and Hispanic Marketing Groups with Online

Multicultural marketing teams essentially compete for budgets with online marketing groups, because these two subsets of marketing have historically been entrepreneurial. While still in the "minority" today, online will become one of the most important channels at the same time that Hispanics will become the ethnic majority by 2050. Looking to the future, management needs to coordinate these two domestic business-growth drivers so that the two areas learn from one another and work together to build successful, living content initiatives online. In terms of incentives, talk to compensation consultants about how to establish incentives to the web and Hispanic marketing teams to work together and test new concepts.

In the white paper *Leaving la Vida Loca*, DePalma says, "Organize across channels, organizations, and geographies. Create ethnic SWAT teams inside your company, crossing organizational boundaries. Involve global teams to leverage translation that may already be underway for Latin American markets. You may find much of what you need already translated for countries south of the border."

For example, DePalma recommends identifying marketing managers responsible for the Hispanic or multicultural segments as well as the Spanish-language websites in Spain, Mexico, and Argentina so that you can share resources, processes, and technology. Spanish-language developers may be hard to find, so it's best to pool resources.

Launch Good Spanish-Language Sites in Tandem

If your company does business in multiple Spanish-language countries (Mexico, Argentina, Spain, etc.) each market should have the same high-quality website. Search engines will notice almost immediately if you launch a well-designed content site in Spanish in the U.S., optimized for search, while your site from Mexico still functions like one from 1998. Consumers will always find the better site and want to browse, shop, or read the content there, no matter where that site resides in the world. Many companies fall into the trap of launching mini-sites or pages for their U.S. Hispanic or foreign markets only to forget about them soon after their launch. Web users fulfill the prophecy of those web-marketing initiatives by not paying attention to the mini-sites that the marketing and web teams do not update. Without any useful, "living" content, the sites won't be used. Local marketing managers can easily provide excuses for such results, so be sure to set goals once websites launch.

Sharing Digital Marketing Practices Worldwide

Digital marketing expertise should be shared among all teams including the general market team, Hispanic marketing team, and country-specific teams. For example, all your colleagues should know how to use Google's tools, such as Analytics, Trends, or Keyword Suggestion to find out what consumers look for online and then how users land on marketers' websites. By using the correct search terms and distribution channel, your SEO strategy can be much better aligned with your CRM and marketing campaign management. For example, perhaps your country-specific marketing teams can learn from your general marketing team how to use digital technologies to tailor their messages to local demographics by IP address or with behavioral targeting. Sharing insights about how to use these technologies can provide incredible competitive advantage in the Hispanic world, where multicultural or international marketing experts typically lack know-how.

Globalization Needs a Champion

The best way for a company to centralize its web initiatives is to put a senior executive in charge with the authority to grow your business online, across borders, as consumers naturally use the web, according to DePalma. Some companies hire a chief globalization officer (CGO) or director of globalization to oversee North American or global web strategy, production of web content, and back-end operations among the U.S. general market, Hispanic market, and Mexican market. A possible workflow, with the CGO overseeing all operations, is shown in the following diagram.

Major Functional Areas Under the Chief Globalization Officer

Technology	Content	Design	Marketing
Architecture	Content catalogs	Usability engineering	Analysis
Spending	Guidelines	Information flow	Campaign design
Tools	Processes	Look and feel	Data collection
Consistency	Testing	Local market adaptation	Cross-channel integration

Source: Business Without Borders, *Donald A. DePalma, Globa Vista Press, 2002–2004, p. 193, Figure 8.3, Major Functional Areas. Used with permission.*

An increasing number of companies focus their globalization efforts on ways to consolidate operations and spending, formalize operations, and leverage investment in core technologies and people, according to DePalma. Why waste time hiring and managing multiple website teams and technology specialists when web efforts can grow and scale out globally? Of course, you need to have local teams in each market that put the frosting on the cake that the central web team bakes. The same is true with translation and localization vendors. Centralize your efforts and then roll out sites on a country-by-country basis.

Alternatively, you can appoint regional or site-specific directors who report to COOs or CMOs with global responsibility for managing web localization efforts, provided that they have the blessing from top executives to improve marketing, technology, and website functionality in each of the target markets.

DePalma, in his book *Business Without Borders*, recommends following the chief globalization officer's six-step process as you expand your web efforts into new domestic (Hispanic) or international markets, leveraging the reach of the web.

1. Find the people to implement your plan and assign responsibilities for each undertaking

2. Specify the technology and tools.

3. Define the content, guidelines, and processes.

4. Design a corporate look and feel, site design and color palettes. Do this in conjunction with the marketing managers, localization professionals, and digital branding experts.

5. Develop the information architecture and site navigation.

6. Get the word out by setting up your online marketing team, analyzing market potential and customer behaviors, design campaigns, and improve the collection and application of data.

U.S. Latino Websites Can Pave the Way for International Expansion

For those visitors who continue to seep into the "wrong" sites despite your best efforts to guide them elsewhere, have no fear. There are ways to turn this to your advantage. "Some companies view domestic multicultural communities as stepping-stones to the countries from which these domestic ethnic buyers came," says DePalma in his book *Business Without Borders*. "Firms have taken this domestic, language-only localization approach to grease the skids for international expansion. As multicultural communities grow both organically and through immigration, these secondary markets will offer an increasing opportunity to grow revenue and share." This opportunity isn't limited to companies based in the United States. Companies in Mexico and even Spain can use the web to test the waters and evaluate demand for their product in the growing U.S. Latino market.

Multicultural Websites as Learning Opportunities

Let's say that your company currently focuses only on the U.S. Hispanic market, but you see that your website content attracts a good number of Mexicans. Perhaps you can welcome these potential customers to your site and find out more regarding why they are visiting. Can you include a short survey on the international splash page? Can these consumers identify new growth markets or even request distribution partners? Suddenly, a U.S. Hispanic marketer could become the international growth hero of a company, identifying new ways to expand beyond the United States, where forecast GDP growth rates will be around 1 percent versus the expected Latin America GDP growth rates of around 5 percent with less competition. Lastly, consider what Latin American immigrants in the United States, with different psychographic motivators, can teach you about how to create campaigns on the worldwide web that will open doors to international markets.

Lessons Learned

- If you consider the web an important sales, marketing or customer service channel, then centralize web technologists into one central group, as Walmart did.
- Don't launch U.S. Hispanic or foreign mini-sites and web initiatives only to forget about them after their launch. They can become a self-fulfilling failure.
- Integrate multicultural and international marketing together with your web team to take advantage of translation and technology investment synergies.
- If you see visitors from Mexico or Latin America on your U.S. Hispanic pages, ask how you can leverage these insights to propose business expansion plans into these markets.
- If your company is based in Mexico or Spain, think about how you can expand virtually or test the waters of the fast-growing U.S. Hispanic market to see what products and services they search for online.

Monster: Managing a Global Brand en Español

By John Hyland
VP and General Manager – Emerging Markets
Monster.com

Monster launched its website for Mexico in 2007. As a U.S.-based business, we wanted to deliberately develop an understanding of the business and online culture in Mexico as well as the overall dynamics of the market before taking a dramatic step into the market. Recruitment is very much a local event. If we want to connect Mexican candidates with Mexican opportunities, we need to thoroughly understand the landscape to do that correctly. Additionally, we needed to learn a lot about the media environment to understand the right vehicles for our business to ensure that we would get the most value from our investments. Starting too big can create expectations that are out of line with what is reasonable. Ultimately trying to move too fast could compromise the long-term success of the business if the investment does not produce the desired results and demonstrable growth.

Cross-Border Visitors

We have significant cross-pollination of visitors from the U.S. and across Latin America to the Mexico site. Some of this fulfills the search needs of users while some of it has to do with a level of immaturity in how differentiation is made across the array of the Spanish-language Internet. About 500,000 unique visitors per month visit our site including 85+ percent in Mexico, 8 percent from Latin America, 2 percent from the U.S., and another 1 percent from Spain.

Managing a Global Web Platform

Monster uses a proprietary technology to distribute job ads through a global network. Those ads are IP-targeted to ensure that what is served is relevant. Navigating from our Monster property to another site is simple for anyone who lands there unintentionally. The Mexico site very specifically supplies information about opportunities within the Mexican market. If a user comes from Argentina or the U.S. with an interest about employment in Mexico, the experience is intended to be the same for them as if they were in Mexico.

We adapt much of our technology platform that we use across the world. In the initial stages, we use mass translation techniques and then localize that translation through the use of native language speakers who assure us that literal translations are replaced with the most recognizable terms for the local audience. Getting it right takes a programmatic approach more than a project approach.

Managing Sites from a Central Office

Monster is a matrixed organization. We have region-based and function-specific reporting lines. Our regional leadership for Latin America in São Paulo supports some key functional areas remotely for both our South and Central America teams. Almost every function is represented in São Paulo, but they still receive support from the corporate office in the U.S. The size of the market and the demands of the responsibilities will determine the structure of that team as it grows. Mexico serves as the hub for Central America and has fewer functional resources in comparison with the São Paulo office. Smaller countries may be staffed primarily as sales offices with limited operational responsibilities.

Challenges of Managing a Global Brand Online

It is a tremendous advantage to have a globally recognized brand. At the same time, we have to be very careful and very diligent about how (and if) we standardize messaging and about how we communicate within each market about our business. The issue of translation *and* localization of language that applies to the site development is even more important and more complex when dealing with brand messaging. Monster in the U.S. has 95%+ brand recognition. We can take some liberties in messaging and taglines because we can safely assume everyone knows who we are and what we do. In a new market, we are in the process of educating our audience about those things. We need to be more explanatory in our messaging to make sure that we can connect with an audience that is not yet familiar with the company. Additionally, our marketing messages in the U.S. often use word play and invoke humor. Many times this simply does not translate to achieve the desired result, or it can even be inappropriate or detrimental. Think of the classic case of trying to market the Chevy Nova in Spanish-language markets. ["No Va" literally means "doesn't go" in Spanish, hence the model from the 1970s was not well received in Latin America.] We have strict brand guidelines, and we try to be as consistent as possible in brand communications; however, we always adapt as needed to make the messages relevant for our state of development within the market and to meet the expectations of our audience.

Growth in Latin America

Latin America is a key focus for our company in 2010 and well beyond. For our industry, the region is still in its infancy, but it is already growing quickly, and the growth is expected to accelerate in the next few years. The big regions in the world that today have a developed market for online recruitment services are North America, Europe, Asia, and Latin America. Monster has an established leadership position in the first three, but not yet in Latin America. As the only truly global business in this industry, this is a situation that we are committed to changing. Building a leadership position in Latin America will allow us to serve existing customers better, acquire new and valuable customers operating in the region, and tap into a wealth of talented candidates that we have not yet been able to reach in a targeted way.

Advice for Other Marketers with a Pan-Regional Brand

I recommend being prudent. It is not just the language that is different; cultures need to be factored in just as much. Additionally, just because the adoption level of the Internet lags behind more-developed markets, that does not mean that the existing users are any less sophisticated or demanding. Putting in place an inferior offering will not drive results. It must be understood that the markets share commonalities, but they are not the same, and the individual differences of Latin American markets have to be considered to avoid taking a one-size-fits-all approach.

Chapter 7

Which "Flavor" of Spanish for the Worldwide Web?

ONCE you decide to launch a Spanish-language website, you need to consider what type of Spanish you should use: universal or neutral Spanish, Latin American Spanish, or a country-specific Spanish. Considering that Spanish-language Internet users have such an amazing propensity to consume content in Spanish from around the world via search, social media, or by visiting sites from their countries of origin, it seems that a universal, or neutral, Spanish would work best on the worldwide web, right?

That can make a great deal of sense especially if you incorporate social networking tools, as Lexicon Marketing does (Chapter 1), or elements of user-generated comments, as Ford does (Chapter 9), where visitors can "personalize" their experience by leaving comments or reviews in whatever form of Spanish they feel comfortable communicating in.

Yet there are many more factors that go into making this decision, including your target market, business objectives, website content, level of formality, and budget.

Three Types of Spanish

Before we explore these numerous factors, let's define the three main types of Spanish.

Universal Spanish

Also known as international or neutral Spanish, this form represents a compromise in terms of terminology and style, as it is not an official language. For example, it avoids local terms and other linguistic idiosyncrasies that can be identified with specific countries (*ordenador,* or "computer" in Spain) or linguistic regions (*vos,* or "you" in Argentina). Universal Spanish is widely used by Microsoft and other computing companies.

> "As long as those compromises are understood and agreed upon by the client, using a neutral Spanish typically works perfectly well and generates considerable cost savings compared to developing and maintaining multiple versions of the same language," says Teddy Bengtsson, the CEO of Idea Factory Languages, a translation and localization company based in Buenos Aires. Approximately 50 percent of his company's work is in universal Spanish.

MotionPoint—a website translation, hosting, and globalization company with clients like Best Buy, Victoria's Secret, Delta, and Domino's—finds that more than 96 percent of the sites that it translates use universal Spanish. The company hosts sites for audiences around the world. According to Chuck Whiteman, senior vice president of MotionPoint, "For the most part, we find our clients have understood this and opt for a universal, non-confrontational Spanish on their websites. Only when clients target a very narrow target market do they opt for a regionally specific variation."

Cost saving can be significant by translating only one website into universal Spanish versus many localized versions. In certain industries, that can work. In others, it cannot. For example, if you are selling cars, it would be easiest to launch one website in Spanish, but the term for "autos" is different in certain markets. (See the list in the table on page 102 for the variations.) In addition, the term for "car dealership" is also different, depending on the region.

Lionbridge, one of the largest translation and localization companies, recommends that its clients use either universal Spanish or divide a translation project into Castilian Spanish for Spain and Latin American Spanish for the Americas when its clients communicate with consumers in a formal tone. In many cases, content can be translated into Latin American Spanish and then adjusted for the Castilian version.

Some companies argue that universal Spanish is not valid for marketing, as it comes across as odd to native Spanish speakers. However, the web draws us all closer together, and the adoption of universal Spanish is more pronounced than ever. Francisco Ceballos, of MercadoLibre, agrees that the Internet is moving toward a universal Spanish just as happened with the English language. But he cautions companies about linguistic challenges, some as fundamental as translating the term "username." In Argentina, it would be *apodo* whereas in Mexico it would be *seudonimo*. MercadoLibre opted for the universally accepted term *usuario* instead.

Latin American Spanish

This neutral, pan-regional Spanish avoids localisms and can be understood in all of the Spanish-speaking countries across the Americas. Similar to universal Spanish, Latin American Spanish also represents a compromise with terminology and style but without the linguistic differences particular to Spain. Bengtsson says that about 30 percent of his company's Spanish projects can be defined as Latin American.

Juan Tornoe, of Hispanic Trending, calls this middle-of-the-road approach "Walter Cronkite Spanish" (Abasto, March 2010), indicating that newscasters and television networks can produce content using Latin American Spanish in Mexico, Venezuela, Los Angeles, or Miami, and everyone will understand it. Even smart advertisers can use it effectively across Latin America.

Because about 90 percent of the world's Spanish-speaking population lives in the Americas, Latin American Spanish can cover a lot of ground, and there is no doubt that the future growth will come from this part of the Spanish-speaking world.

Country-Specific Spanish

This version of Spanish obviously requires the greatest amount of work and investment because of the level of customization involved. At the same time, it can also yield the greatest return by incorporating more localisms and having a higher degree of cultural relevance. When marketers use "culturally sensitive" content, as is often the case with advertising, Bengtsson recommends always performing a test in the target market to ensure that the translation has the appropriate linguistic and cultural nuances. Only 20 percent of his company's workload for Spanish relates to country-specific projects, the majority for Spain. Spain, while being a more mature and stable economy, represents only 10 percent of the Spanish-speaking global audience.

Lionbridge recommends using country-specific flavors of Spanish for marketing messages with an informal tone. Alternatively, when clients do not have the budget for multiple translations, Lionbridge suggests breaking up localization projects into three flavors: One for the U.S. Hispanic, Puerto Rican and Mexican markets; a second for Argentina and Uruguay to incorporate the personal pronoun *vos; and* a third for the remaining Latin American countries including Peru, Costa Rica, Ecuador, El Salvador, Colombia, Venezuela, and Chile. Either Colombian, Ecuadorian, or Costa Rican flavors of Spanish can work, as these countries have a reputation for speaking in a neutral tone, clearly understood by a large variety of Spanish speakers.

Here are examples of the differences in Spanish, some of which highlight regional differences and slang among their respective countries:

English	Spain	Argentina	Mexico	Chile	Costa Rica
hard disk	disco duro	disco rígido	disco duro	disco duro	disco duro
swimming pool	piscina	pileta	alberca	piscine	piscina
swimsuit	bañador	malla	traje de baño	traje de baño	traje de baño
ticket	billete	boleto	boleto	boleto	boleto
to enter	introducir	ingresar	ingresar	introducir	meter / introducir
car	coche	auto	carro / coche	auto	carro / auto
call	llamada	llamado	llamada	llamada	llamada
money	pasta	plata	lana	plata	plata
boy	chaval	pibe	plebe / huerquillo	cabro	chiquito / niño
eat	papear	morfar	taquear	zampar	comer
are you stupid?	¿eres gilipollas, tío?	¿sos boludo, che?	¿estás pendejo?	¿eres huevón?	¿eres huevón?
be worn-out	estoy molido/ reventado	estoy roto	estoy traqueteado	estoy molido	estoy molido

Source: Lionbridge

In addition to the differences in vocabulary, the following areas need to be customized prior to any localization project: currency, time and date formats, decimal separators, units of measurement, and capitalization.

How to Decide Which Type of Spanish

Now that we have defined the three "types" of Spanish, let's take a closer look at the factors to consider for making your decision: target market, level of formality, and budget.

Understand Your Target Market's Language

On the worldwide web, while you may *intend* to reach only U.S. Hispanics or Mexicans online, you may be surprised by the degree to which you attract a worldwide audience, even when you do not expect to serve international customers. That is why it is critical to clearly define your target market and use all of the tools to localize your website. Or you can choose to cast a wider net and draw in that international audience, if that is your goal.

"Consumers around the world really seem to seek out the best content on the web, and they often find it on U.S. websites," says Whiteman, of MotionPoint. "When you think about the investment that most large U.S. companies make in their websites, it's really not that surprising that a high-quality U.S. website draws a global audience."

So, while you may define your target market online as the U.S. Hispanic market only, you may want to consider using universal Spanish to broaden the potential revenue opportunities into Mexico to include shoppers who cross the border. In addition, once you see the demand coming from outside of the United States, you may want to consider a more comprehensive global strategy that goes beyond Spanish.

Using a localization and translation vendor with solid technology can provide a deeper understanding of where your site visitors come from and their online behavior. This can both help you refine your target market and help you identify where to consider expanding your business virtually.

MotionPoint finds that 80 to 90 percent of the typical website is composed of the same basic content regardless of the market being served. Technology can reduce the amount of time and money spent translating this content into Spanish. These savings allow companies to focus their scarce resources on customizing and testing the most heavily trafficked content. It also frees resources that can be better used actually driving Hispanic traffic to the website. For companies trying to serve Hispanics online, MotionPoint counsels its clients to apply the 80/20 rule. First translate the site into Spanish and then optimize the 20 percent of the site that drives 80 percent of its value. Companies that take this approach typically generate a higher return on their investment as well as reduce the complexity and time-to-market of their translated websites.

Level of Formality

Your brand may want to provide information to adults in a formal tone or perhaps reach teenagers who use a lot of slang. The intended audience may help you determine what kind of Spanish to use. Obviously, in Spanish, you can use either *usted*, the formal "you"; *tu*, the friendly, informal "you"; or alternatively the plural forms including *ustedes*, formal for the plural "you" in English, and *vosotros*, used only in Spain, for the informal, plural form of "you." Your choice will be based on whether you are trying to make a personal connection with your customers or to respect the distance between you and them. In general, it may be a safer bet to use the more-formal *usted*, especially if you allow users to personalize their experience by writing reviews and leaving comments.

In answering the question "What is language for multilinguals?" on her blog, Nathalie Molina, at Lionbridge, describes Spanish as the emotional language that she learned during her childhood, or "the linguistic fetal position that brings comfort and sanity when everything else fails." In contrast, English is the language of structure, learning, and business. "Bottom line, language is inextricably tied to culture and emotions," she wrote. As marketers, do you want to make an emotional, more personal connection with your consumers using the language of their culture? Or does your product or campaign aim to maintain a respectful distance?

Budget

The more types of Spanish translation or content development you need, the more expensive your website(s) will be. In addition, as online audiences grow in Latin America, the need to launch individual sites in each country will increase, which will increase budgets significantly but at the same time achieve more targeted results. In any case, as you develop your web-marketing strategies, you need to keep your online marketing budget aligned with the growing, changing needs of the market. Two areas to keep your eye on in the future may help you either keep costs down or allow you to experiment with web projects in Spanish: outsourcing translations and crowdsourcing translations.

Outsourcing Translations

It may not make sense to hire a domestic translator or even a developer if you can obtain similar or identical results for approximately half the price in Argentina or Costa Rica. Across Latin America, Argentina has become an outsourcing hub for translation of all types of Spanish as well as web and software development. MercadoLibre located its two development centers in Argentina due to the tax incentives that the company receives in return.

Because of the high number of well-educated, highly skilled professionals with a hunger for opportunity, Teddy Bengtsson started his translation and localization company, Idea Factory Languages, in Buenos Aires. The combination of good infrastructure, skilled translators, and a relatively good number of programmers and web experts with low labor rates make countries like Argentina a good bet.

Regarding the idea of outsourcing editorial in Spanish to markets with lower labor costs like Argentina (for Spanish) or India (for English), Jon Stross, BabyCenter's vice president of U.S. Hispanic and international sales, strongly advises hiring local editorial teams in each country that know local practices. In the case of his company, local staff better understand the health care systems and the different baby-related and pregnancy terms in each country.

In addition, be careful to culturally adjust, translate, or change product names as this "FARTFULL" example from IKEA shows. Verify translations with multiple native speakers and make sure product names don't come across as inappropriate. You may find that some names come across differently in English than they do in Swedish, for example.

Crowdsourcing Translations

Facebook's translation via crowdsourcing provides a good example of a game-changing, technological innovation that can bring new web services to market much more quickly and cost-effectively. While crowdsourcing shows great promise for applications outside of Facebook, it also presents challenges and requires that companies accept a higher tolerance for risk. Crowdsourcing, as the word implies, combines the concept of outsourcing projects to the "crowd," or masses. This can apply to computer programming or in this case, to translating.

One of the obvious benefits of crowdsourcing is speed. It took only one week for Facebook's volunteer translators to translate its site into Spanish, its second language after English, and only 24 hours for French. In comparison, the traditional model of translating a site seems costly and completely unscalable, according to Ghassan Haddad, the director of localization at Facebook.

After speed, the second obvious benefit is reach. By tapping into the collective desire of a community to translate a user interface into its native language (with solid technology), Facebook successfully grew its audience globally by involving its users in the translation process. And, with hundreds of millions of users, Facebook can extend the reach of its site via crowdsourcing to all Internet users, including speakers of commonly ignored languages.

A third benefit could be cost savings, but Haddad says that the investment in technology offsets some of the savings attained by getting "free" translations. In addition, the community translations undergo extensive quality assurance testing by professional agencies, so that adds costs. Nevertheless, cost advantages can be achieved through delivering users' translations of normally unsupported languages, automating the process of translating the site, and prioritizing text during the translation process.

There are certain benefits to crowdsourcing that could not be achieved through traditional means. For example, imagine the translation of new social media terms like "wall-to-wall," "poke," "It's complicated" (referring to a relationship) or "tag" (a person in a photo). Perhaps users have the best ideas for how to translate these 21st century terms compared with an official translator.

Yet there remain obvious concerns about the quality of crowdsourced translations. According to Haddad, high-quality translations accurately convey the original meaning of the text, do not sound like a translation, and result in clear and unambiguous copy. So how do you get there? To achieve high-quality translations, companies must employ the right combination of people, process, and technology. The people must be linguistically competent and experts in the milieu of social networks; the process must facilitate speed and quality; and the technology must enable the implementation of process with as little friction as possible. The crowdsourced translations on Facebook include a five-part process: detailed glossaries and style guides in each language, voting during the translation process by users (thumbs up or thumbs down), verification, quality assurance, and release of the translated user interface to the public.

Some of the challenges that Haddad faced include:

- Keeping the community interested and engaged during the initial translation and maintenance phases
- Availability of enough contributors to complete the translation, especially when working with "unsupported" languages
- Ensuring acceptable quality in all languages
- Reusing already translated terms
- Technical issues such as access, scalability, control, and security
- Highly dynamic nature of text and complexity of some languages
- Predictability

In conclusion, always check the quality of a crowdsourced translation with a translator or native speaker.

The Best Example of Crowdsourced Translations: TED.com

TED is a conference devoted to "Ideas Worth Spreading," which brings leaders together from the technology, entertainment, and design worlds, hence the three-letter acronym. You can find some of the most inspiring, interesting and educational videos on the web on TED.com's archive of video-taped presentations from its sold-out conference with speakers like Al Gore, Elizabeth Gilbert, Malcolm Gladwell, Gary Vaynerchuk, Tim Berners-Lee and James Cameron.

The English-language presentations inspire viewers to such a degree that an ever-increasing group, now nearing 4,400 volunteers, has subtitled the TED Talks into 75 languages in order to share the videos with their native countrymen. Over 630 Spanish translators make it the leading language for subtitled videos on TED.com. The back-end collaborative translation technology for TED is powered by dotSub, as well as by video providers like Adobe, Brightcove, Cisco, Electronic Arts, Intel, Sony, and the U.S. Army, rendering multiple language subtitles for videos on the web and mobile devices, as well as transcription and video editing systems. In the case of TED.com, dotSub has enabled a total of nearly 9,400 translated videos. The most active member is MaYoMo.com, who has translated over 400 talks into Bulgarian and Russian. Anour Dafa-

Alla takes second place, having translated over three hundred talks into Arabic.

Michael Smolens, dotSub's CEO, has spent time with both of them. Anour is from Sudan and lives in Korea while MaYoMo has a small team of people, based in Prague, who work with him on his translations. "Both Anour and MaYoMo translate the content so that their fellow countrymen can experience the power of TED with accurate translations as they feel it is the most inspirational, educational, and transformative content on the web," Smolens says. "In the first year since launching the subtitled versions of the videos on TED.com, views from outside the U.S. increased 350% overall and by 1000% in Latin America, so it is a very easy, inexpensive way to get one's message out in multiple languages to billions of people who before had no access to that content."

What Do the Readers Say?

Eduardo Arcos was born in Ecuador, lived in Mexico City for 10 years, and currently splits his time between Belgium and Spain. He's a global citizen. After founding his blog network, Hipertextual, and its lead technology news site, ALT1040, millions of (mostly) young men around the Spanish-language world have come to follow his and his team's blog posts from Spain, Mexico, Argentine, Peru, and the United States.

The entry below from his personal blog in October 2009 captures the essence of the question about what Spanish to use.

A Spanish More Appropriate for Latin America

(Excerpt from Eduardo Arcos's blog, October 2009, translated from the Spanish)

> A few minutes ago, we received an email at info@hipertextual.com from a person congratulating us for our blogs but at the same time complaining about the type of Spanish that we use on our site, especially for the liberal translation of some terms in English, "in general, a Spanish that is more appropriate for Latin America."

This person lives in Spain and although his email is respectful and states that he does not undervalue the Spanish from "the other side of the pond," it annoyed him (contextually reading into his message) to read posts with this type of Spanish.

Calling into question then the form in which we ought to write blogs, is the editor's own style valid if so many people become annoyed with a "strange" Spanish compared to what they are used to? During the ten years that I have written blogs, I've read opinions in favor and against the use of words like "ordenador" (computer, in Spain) or "computadora" (computer, in Latin America), and although for me it's all the same if we use one or the other, it appears that for some people this really matters.

Do you believe that we should have a rule of thumb about the words or writing style to take local customs into consideration at the time that we write? In other words, should we make Spanish more neutral online?

My personal opinion is that localisms (without exaggerating) define our own writing style and a few linguistic exaggerations are fair and at times necessary to define our own style.

Following is a snapshot of the most insightful comments that Eduardo received:

The general rule (I suppose) is to use the "Spanish" of the author of the post, right? This is the Internet and each person has their way of communicating, or their point, which reflects their perspective and where they come from. (Viperhoot on October 27, 2009)

To neutralize a language is to kill its essence. Don't "standardize" words. (Thelma on November 10, 2009)

Eduardo, I just arrived in Madrid and Barcelona, even though I try to understand everything about this matter of language, for the Spaniards it is such a big issue. I'm Ecuadorian and I feel proud of Latin American Spanish. I believe that ALL of us 569 million Latin Americans ought to value our own diversity and openness, the dynamism of our language. From this point of view, I read that this trauma of the Spaniards has its origin in the nationalism of Franco's regime. Please Eduardo, don't change your style; the Spaniards defend their identity to such a degree that they ask us to abandon ours which is more open, and more universal in the end. (Mario on November 1, 2009)

I am writing from Spain: The most important thing about a language is that we can understand. Do you understand this person that you are reading? Then what gives? It seems that this position is like being a "Taliban of language." (Jose Alberto on November 8, 2009)

It's perfectly fine that you use localisms. In this way it's easy to identify where editors come from and on what they base their opinions. Trying to use a neutral Spanish doesn't make sense. To blog is to define your style and if we all use the same type of Spanish, not only does it sound strange, but it's improper. I'm in favor of each blogger writing his or her entries in the Spanish that they best know how to write in. (Damian on November 8, 2009)

As the song says, "be yourself no matter what they say." As you say, this affects every person that has his or her own writing style. The norm ought to be that every person writes as is natural to him or her. I remember a get-together in Tampa, FL ten years ago. There was a dinner party with people from all over the world: Cubans, Venezuelans, Puerto Ricans, Dominicans, Argentineans, Ecuadorians and Peruvians. There weren't that many but there were people from all over the world from virtually every Spanish-speaking country. And there was a woman from Bilbao that lived in Madrid, who was vacationing for 3 months in Tampa. She was the only one among us who didn't understand the rest of us, everything seemed odd. A coincidence? (Frank November 8, 2009)

I believe that I have a solution for Eduardo. How would it be if we put language support and every person could select what kind of Spanish the reader wants? For example, you could have Castilian, Mexican, Argentinean, Colombian, etc. Truth be told, I've never gotten upset about a blog post that uses the local language of the author. Does the same happen between the English with North Americans, Australians, Indians or South Africans? (Julio F on November 9, 2009)

I love it when you touch about themes like this one in your posts! One time my readers told me that the language I use on my blog had too many localisms from Spain, which I use so that people in Barcelona, where I have lived since I was four years old can understand. Of course, when I speak with people from Mexico, it makes for humorous situations and vice versa. Because of that, I believe the following. One, I hate it when someone considers Castilian (Spanish from Spain) better than Spanish and distinguishes the first as the language that they speak in Spain and the second that we speak in Latin America. Two, it's inevitable to mix (in the oral or the written) if you are part of two worlds. But of course, the flavors break apart into different types in each of our heads in this world. ;) (mariana m on November 23, 2009)

I find these comments especially relevant for a few reasons. First, more and more companies enable social media features like commenting to connect with consumers on their websites, so the theme of empowering users to speak in their own Spanish on blog posts is important to understand.

Second, the United States isn't the only country that is becoming more multicultural; the whole world is. The comments responding to his post capture the pros, cons, and ongoing battle of deciding what type of Spanish works best for the web, especially among consumers, all of whom share a passion around one common theme, consumer technology, but live in disparate countries.

You can discuss what type of Spanish you ought to use, but, ultimately, consumer feedback rules. While the comments respond to the differences between Spanish from Spain versus Latin America, this provides a template where you can replace "Puerto Rican" or "Mexican" for the other countries of origin mentioned here.

Which Spanish Is Right for My Brand?

In his book, *The Power of Business en Español*, Jose Cancela says, "The commonly held belief that we have to speak different forms of Spanish to communicate with Hispanics in different parts of the U.S.A. is just not true. It's a myth. It's people making things harder than they have to be."

Increasingly, it appears that the same is true of Spanish on the web. Users, especially in Latin America, discover Spanish-language websites from around the world because of search and a shortage of content in their local markets. In addition, the United States attracts English and

Spanish speakers globally as a focal point of entertainment, fashion, business, and commerce.

Cost–Benefit Analysis

When you do a cost–benefit analysis to determine how many Spanish-language translations or complete websites in Spanish you want to invest in, consider how each will accomplish your business goals. Before you jump into using universal or Latin American Spanish because of the cost savings, carefully consider the nuances of the terminology within your industry, product, or brand, and ask how the terminology is communicated in each market in which you do business. Listen to your users, as in Arcos's blog post. Launching local, country-specific sites with customized translations (or entirely new content), while being the most expensive option, may deliver the message that is most understood in-market.

Most importantly, offering a translation of your website in Spanish is far better than having nothing at all. With even a small investment, Latino consumers will greatly appreciate your efforts in identifying their needs and communicating with them.

Latino*Link*

Find a translator online:
http://www.proz.com/
http://www.atanet.org/
http://www.gala-global.org

Lessons Learned

- Evaluate the linguistic nuances among the different forms of Spanish relative to the vocabulary of your industry and product lines.
- Universal Spanish may be the cheapest because it requires the fewest customized localizations and provides the largest reach on the web.
- Localizing your web copy into more local variants of Spanish can yield a greater degree of clarity, but it costs more.
- Consider emotional and cultural ties to the Spanish language.
- Find the right translation and localization partner that can help

you share some of the risk and get your translated site to market quickly.

- Keep an eye on new technologies that enable crowdsourced translations. This presents an area of opportunity for those companies that are willing to accept the risks associated with it.

- Listen to consumer feedback regarding the Spanish you use on your site.

- Provide the necessary field support and customer service in Spanish to accompany your translated website.

- Last, social networking features on your site may allow different forms of Spanish to exist at the same time, especially for user reviews and comments.

Developing an Online Latino Identity: AmFamLatino.com

By Jose A. Rivera
Web Experience Manager
American Family Insurance

Background

American Family Insurance first launched its Spanish-language web presence in 2005 as a section within the newly redesigned www.amfam.com. It focused on high-level products and services without any location-specific pages or tools.

In 2006, our research showed that, by adding more Spanish-language content, we could drive growth in our target DMAs like Chicago, Phoenix, and Milwaukee, among others. We added content through a manual process of sending individual pages to translation companies, then on to legal and then back to the web team for integration. As our content and traffic grew, we started to offer sales and service applications in Spanish as well and thus created amfamlatino.com. This provides an identity and platform to communicate our connection to Latinos online. While other websites only add "español" to their general market sites, we felt that it was important to give our Spanish website its own identity.

Providing Information, Building Trust

Insurance is based upon trust, or being there when needed. Being new in a country, learning a new language, and not having a clear understanding about how insurance works requires us to offer as much information as possible to our users about our company and services. Many Latinos do not feel comfortable calling an insurance agent whom they have never met, let alone walking into an agency if they are unsure whether the personnel speak Spanish. For this reason, www.amfamlatino.com offers tools that allow our users to educate themselves about insurance before taking the next step: completing a purchase. Our Agent Locator application enables users to select an agent that speaks their native language.

When a web tool rolls out in English, it appears in Spanish as well, as a requirement. So, we do not take a phased approach to language. Hispanic users have demonstrated the fastest growth online, and they look for content and tools in their language of choice.

Today, we are proud to have more than 85 percent of our general market website translated into Spanish, which includes our account management tools, billing applications, the agent locator, and sales tools for auto and property insurance. Having a complete, in-language website minimizes users switching to the English-language site and ultimately provides a better user experience.

The American Dream

Our brand proposition is "Family First and Forward," which resonates with Hispanic families that work hard to obtain the things they own and reach the American Dream. We begin our relationship with our customers by explaining in plain language (not insurance talk) the importance of insurance because, in many Latin American countries, insurance is not required.

We offer tools such as the Interactive Home to teach consumers who have never had exposure to insurance which products may best fit their life stage and lifestyle. Auto insurance is a "gateway" product, and we understand that most Hispanics are price sensitive. Our call to action is to get a quote online, while offering the high touch of a local agent. This differs from some competitors who base their business model on price, with minimal local representation. This is particularly important to Latino customers who need to trust someone in a new country who not only speaks their language but also understands their cultural background.

The Translation Process

At first, we used different translation vendors in a manual process, resulting in long production times even with limited content updates. Most translation companies do not directly work on HTML pages. So our web team used to copy all the content into three-column Microsoft Word documents labeled: Original Content, Spanish Translation, and English Back-Translation. A native Spanish speaker would translate the first column into the second one. Then a different translator whose first language is English would translate back to validate the Spanish content.

This is a common practice but, in my opinion, is not effective. I saw more mistakes in the back translation than in the original because of the difficulty in translating some concepts. The legal department often rejected the translation document, causing the web team to start the process over again. Once the content was approved, the web developers would create new HTML pages based on the Microsoft Word document. Five web pages could require anywhere from five days to two weeks to translate.

Because of this laborious process, we began working with Motion-Point, which offers an automated approach to web page translation. This company's solution allows us to maintain only one website and base the new Spanish content around it. Any time we deploy new content in English, MotionPoint's system detects it and sends it to a translation queue. The process takes it to a translator, an editor, and a proofreader before it becomes available for approval. Native speakers who have experience in the field they are servicing, in our case financial products, translate the content. The translated content is saved in a database as complete sentences. If the system detects a sentence in English, it replaces it with the pre-translated Spanish content. This is a real-time process: The customer requests a page in Spanish, and the system intercepts the page and inserts a "language layer" before delivering the final page. Other benefits of working with an automated solution are that only new content is translated. If the statement has been previously translated, we are not charged for it.

MotionPoint worked with us in establishing a glossary of terms and outlining which words were translatable and which were not, such as branded terms. Another benefit is that all translations are certified and the liability for the translation is transferred to the vendor. Because of this, a back translation is no longer necessary. To improve consistency between web and printed material, we all use the same solution. This way print benefits from pre-translated web content and vice versa.

Determining What "Flavor" of Spanish to Use
We knew that we wanted to use "Universal Spanish." We understand that in our operating states the highest concentrations of Latinos are Mexican descent. However, our website reaches other segments of the U.S Hispanic population, and because of this we must consider not using col-

loquialisms or "slang" that may be specific to a nationality. When defining the "flavor" of Spanish, the education level is most important. Insurance by nature is a complex concept, and it is even more difficult to comprehend if you are being introduced to it for the first time using the Internet, which could be impersonal. Our Spanish translation is based on an eighth-grade-level education—not because our online users are not educated beyond that level but to ensure that it is as clear and transparent as possible. There is some terminology that can't be simplified too much in order for it to be concise. To support difficult topics, we encourage the use of FAQs—insurance guides for Auto, Home and Life—as well as always making the presence of our American Family agents felt throughout the website for more information. As a company, we may do targeted executions for TV, print, events, and sponsorships supported by media buys in areas dominated by a specific ethnicity, but we feel that making language, imagery, and call to actions appeal to the general Latino public is more effective both from an economical and brand awareness standpoint.

Geographic Targeting

American Family operates in 19 states. While most of our traffic comes from those operating states, we also see traffic from states where we do not have a presence. This may be due to search engines and other national advertising efforts that reach a wider market. Midwestern states like Wisconsin, Illinois, Minnesota, and Missouri represent approximately 40 percent of our general market traffic because, for more than 80 years, we have served policyholders there.

In Spanish, the largest activity comes from Arizona, Colorado, Illinois, and Georgia. U.S. Hispanics adopt technology more quickly compared with the general market, and this could mean that future incoming website traffic could originate from a mobile device rather than a personal computer.

We geo-target digital campaigns to support traditional advertising efforts. This is not limited to landing pages; it is also used to customize web content based on the origin of an IP address in micro-sites, banners, and home page features. This helps us to align media plans with specific products that target specific states or DMAs as well as pilot digital initiatives.

We offer state-specific information to make sure that the correct coverage information appears accurately in addition to validating location before allowing users to request an insurance estimate.

We make product information relevant using geo-targeting/location and featuring different products on the home page and interior pages than we would feature for the general market or other segmented markets such as Asian or African American.

Promoting the Site

Organic, local, and paid search have produced well for AmFamLatino.com. We invest a great amount of time to make sure that our web pages are optimized. Branded entertainment also had a positive effect on our website. In the past 12 months, we saw that 37 percent of amfam.com and amfamlatino.com visitors were new.

Field and Customer Support

Each of our 4,000 agents gets its own website and Facebook page. Our agents can direct users to their own websites via online banners, which often appear on relocation websites, realty websites, building associations, and sites for business owners. In addition, agents can promote their sites via our self-service kiosks located in shopping malls, auto dealerships, and DMVs. [Author's note: After entering my contact information into the form on American Family Insurance's Spanish-language website, I received a call only four hours later.]

Our English and Spanish call center staff, managed internally, support online questions, quotes by phone, billing and claims. Our claims-specific call centers also have bilingual staff and operate 24/7.

Metrics for Success

We measure success in different ways: brand awareness, purchase consideration, estimates completed, estimates sent to agents, quotes completed, and quotes submitted to agents. Our sales-related tools go through a sales match process. In this way, we compare new business premiums to online activity such as increases in web traffic, time on site, pages consumed and fallout rate.

There are a few things we've learned in our journey of creating the most complete Spanish website by U.S. insurance carriers. Updating the site is an ongoing process and one that is never done. We update the home page quarterly, and every month we launch new micro-sites.

Tips for Launching Your Website in Spanish

- Avoid translating websites internally. Even if you have native speakers working on your site, this exposes your company to liability for translations. Instead, work with partners that can provide certified translations with notarized statements of accuracy, and make them responsible for your multilingual content.

- Establish cross-channel integration. Users expect you to have an integrated approach. If you have a multilingual website, make sure that you have the customer service support for offline issues as well.

- When linked content is not available in languages other than English, let users know. Many times there are reference links to PDFs, external websites, and tools that are not in other languages. A simple "Disponible solo en Ingles" (available only in English) sets the expectation and prevents dissatisfaction that could result in visitors abandoning your site.

- Make imagery relevant: Do not translate content only—also make sure that the images used in the site reflect the segment of the population you are targeting.

- If you have translated contact forms, make sure that you have staff that not only speaks Spanish but is also proficient in reading and writing. Many times this is not verified and some second- or third-generation Hispanics may speak the language but do not have the grammar skills required to respond.

- Verify the best way to address your online users. Formal or informal? This relates to the use of "*tú*" (informal "you") versus "*usted*" (formal "you"). Younger generations may accept "*tú*" while older users may be offended by how casually they are being addressed and prefer "*usted.*"

Chapter 8

Localizing Your Website for Latinos

WHILE translating a website is often the first step in reaching Latinos online, you must consider how to localize your website. Ultimately, localization means making the website look and feel as if it were developed for users in a particular language and culture. In some cases, as exemplified by the Best Buy case study, you may find that U.S. Hispanic users want the Spanish-language site to look and read the same as the English-language site, mirroring the same offers and appearance with a direct translation. In others, as with the Ford case study in Chapter 9, you may find that U.S. Latinas want a customized site for themselves.

John Yunker, co-founder of Byte Level Research and author of *Beyond Borders: Web Globalization Strategies*, shares a few basics about how to localize websites. First, he often reminds his clients that the Internet connects computers whereas language connects people. Second, translation represents only about 10 percent of the localization process. Yunker uses the graphic at right to highlight the different steps in localizing and customizing a website.

As mentioned in Chapter 3, that while intended for U.S. Hispanics, both Best Buy's and The Home Depot's Spanish-language e-commerce sites became popular pan-regionally in Latin America. Any really good content site in Spanish will automatically attract U.S. Hispanics while allowing marketers to virtually enter Latin America at the same time. With that in mind, let's outline six specific ways that marketers can steer consumers to country- and language-specific websites to reach the desired audience and maintain greater control. Next, we will look at how cultural customization of your site goes beyond simply translating content into Spanish, and we'll look at a case study of one company that has accomplished this. Finally, we will leave you with a four-step process of how to best localize and globalize your site.

Localizing Your Website for Latinos

Before the planning and implementation phases of launching a U.S. Hispanic site, you need to decide the ways in which you will direct visitors to the right sites and these decisions must be coordinated between the IT/web and multicultural/international marketing teams.

Global Gateways

The first way to draw Spanish speakers to country- or language-specific sites is to develop global gateways, or landing pages, like this one from Procter & Gamble's Pampers brand. It asks consumers which country-specific site they would like to visit.

Pampers speaks to moms around the world—each country appears in the dominant language of that country, not in English.

John Yunker suggests following three rules when using global gateways: Place function above beauty, don't make users think about what language or country they need to select, don't pretend to speak languages that you don't.

Nike Running's global gateway places one running shoe at the center of its page, in the screen shot on the right, communicating that Nike "speaks running" at its core. Users select their language first and their country second. The site allows runners to keep track of their training schedules and con-

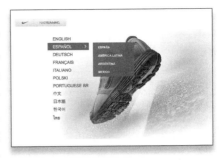

nect with like-minded running enthusiasts in their local communities in Nike+'s proprietary social network. Nike could easily add a link for "Estados Unidos" in the "Español" language category.

Wikipedia's global gateway, on the right, structures itself solely around language, suggesting that it may not matter where you live on the web as long as you can get the information you want in the language you prefer.

Español, Not Spanish

This global gateway at right from Banco Popular offers users a bilingual website in each country in which it does business. Notice how the pages read "Español" not "Spanish." In other words, always put yourself in the shoes of the user.

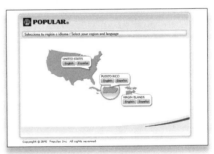

Toggle Buttons

Banco Popular's toggle buttons in this screen shot—for both region and language—appear on the upper right side of the page. From a usability and consistency perspective, this works best. Users expect toggle buttons to appear on the upper right throughout the entire website.

Geo-Location

Use geo-location, or Internet Protocol (IP) targeting, based on the geographic location of the consumer. Best Buy serves this geo-targeted

welcome page to users outside of the United States, which asks them what language they would like to continue in. The page also explains that visitors can order online using international credit cards and either ship those orders to a U.S. addresses or pick them up at a U.S. store. This sets very clear customer expectations with helpful information about where and how customers can pick up their orders.

Yunker says, "Keep in mind that users travel abroad and use shared computers, so you have to be careful when making assumptions about their language and country preference. A website should always have a global gateway so users can override whatever language or country you have presented to them."

For example, imagine taking a vacation to the Riviera Maya in Mexico, opening your laptop and visiting Google.com to find that you are automatically redirected to Google.com.mx, its Mexican site in Spanish. Then, you try visiting Facebook and notice that the default language of your Facebook page has changed to Spanish. This exemplifies two important backend technologies called content and language negotiation.

Content negotiation can deliver specific image or video files to a web browser based on inputs from a user's computer, such as what operating system or version of a web browser users have installed on their computers. Language negotiation, a subset of content negotiation, detects what country a user visits from or what language preference a user has set within the user's browser and then delivers, for example, the Spanish-language version of a website.

Both Google and Facebook use geo-location, or the IP address of the user's current location, to deliver the most customized content and advertising to the greatest number of users, including preferred language that corresponds to the country the user visits from.

"There are different schools of thought when it comes to blocking content online. Some think that it is better to manage user expectations, but there are also good reasons to allow users, regardless of where they come from, to access content. This is mainly because of its potential to improve search engine rankings and cross-linking between websites," says Jose Rivera, the web experience manager at American Family Insurance.

Overall, geo-location, in combination with content and language negotiation, can effectively "guess" what language users want and deliver the most relevant web content to them automatically. More specifically, Hispanic or Latin American users can be better segmented by delivering distinct Spanish-language versions of your website with the above methods.

Jump Pages

A jump page tells users when they are about to leave a page in their preferred language to go to a page in another language. Two types of jump pages can quickly and effectively explain a change in user experience, avoiding confusion among users who prefer having a completely Spanish-language experience online or click to visit partner sites. This pop-up window from Bank of America, which reads, "to continue in English" in the title bar, notifies Spanish-language users that they've clicked on a link that is available only in English.

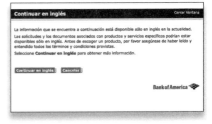

Another type of jump page is this one from Best Buy's Spanish-language site, which explains how users will be "redirected to a site from one of our trusted partners. The information on this site may not be available in Spanish."

These two types of jump pages, while simple to implement, can be very helpful to users, especially among Spanish-preferring Hispanics, many of whom may be new to using the Internet.

Flags Only Represent Countries, Not Languages

Marketers should only use flags on websites that offer country-specific content, like this one from MercadoLibre, which operates websites in each of these countries. Never use flags to denote language.

Culturally Customizing Your Website

While translating your websites into Spanish may be a good first step, you may need to go further to customize and localize your sites to target U.S. Latinos and Latin Americans. Here, we will define five cultural values of what makes a culturally customized website and then we will take a look at a specific example of how Procter & Gamble culturally customized a website for U.S. Latina girls.

Cultural customization begins where basic translation and localization ends according to Dr. Nitish Singh. Experts in the localization industry, like Singh, often recommend developing entirely new sites that incorporate the perceptions, symbols, and behavior of the target market. You can culturally adapt websites and uniquely position your products to Latino audiences by connecting to their culture and values and using the appropriate graphics, pictures and colors.

In their book, *The Culturally Customized Website*, Dr. Singh and Dr. Pereira analyze website content based on a list of five unique cultural values for understanding website design.

- **Individualism versus collectivism:** A belief in importance of the goals of the individual versus the goals of the group.
- **Power distance:** A belief in authority and hierarchy (high power distance) versus the belief that power should be distributed (low power distance).
- **Uncertainty avoidance:** The importance of predictability, structure, and order (high uncertainty avoidance) versus a willingness to take risks and an acceptance of ambiguity and limited structure (low uncertainty avoidance). U.S. Hispanics tend to have a low tolerance

for uncertainty, view conflict and competition as threatening, and value security over adventure and risk.

- **Masculinity versus femininity:** A belief in achievement and ambition (masculine) versus a belief in nurturing and caring for others (feminine).

- **Low versus high context:** High-context cultures have close connections among group members, where little information is explicit and instead symbols and nonverbal cues are used and meanings are embedded in the situational context. In contrast, low-context cultures are logical, linear, and action-oriented. The majority of information is explicit and formalized. Most of the communication in such cultures takes place in a rational, verbal, and explicit way to convey concrete meanings.

Source: The Culturally Customized Web Site: Customizing Web Sites for the Global Marketplace *by Nitish Singh and Arun Pereira. Four of the five cultural values above were developed by Dr. Geert Hofstede in his book* Culture's Consequences: International Differences in Work-related Values. *Used with permission.*

Using these five values, if we compare the U.S. general market with the U.S. Hispanic market, these two groups tend to fall on opposite ends in four of the five categories:

	U.S. General Market	U.S. Hispanics/Latinos
Individualism vs. collectivism	Individualistic	Collectivistic
Power distance	Low power distance	High power distance
Uncertainty avoidance	Low uncertainty avoidance	High uncertainty avoidance
Masculine / Feminine	Masculine	Masculine
Low versus high context	Low context	High context

With this in mind, it is best to study and learn from successful websites from other areas of the Latino world, and then reapply and adapt them to your specific target market. While the text and photos may change on the surface, the underlying cultural values underneath the big idea will most often still be in alignment.

Let's take a look at a specific example of how Procter & Gamble rolled out one branded web initiative targeting teen girls—BeingGirl.com—for its Always and Tampax brands. Here, you will see how the website is culturally customized for its different audiences. At the same time, P&G maintains the image of the brand throughout all of those iterations on the web.

The U.S. general market site for Being Girl (left) includes an option for "Your Period" on the left navigation bar and says in the middle of the page, "Learn and share about growing up and puberty while having fun playing girl games and listening to the latest teen music." The articles and "Ask Iris' Experts" content sections feature straightforward questions with equally straightforward and direct advice, reflecting the low context culture of the United States.

In contrast, the BeingGirl site for English-preferring Hispanic girls—SoloDeChikas.com—does not mention periods, boyfriends, or any straightforward questions. Very little explicit information is shared in the screen shot shown here. Instead, the cultural cues and meanings are embedded in the situational context. Even though the site is in English, the content very much reflects the high-context information preferences among Latinos. In addition, if you compare and contrast the details of the content on Being-Girl.com you will notice how the articles about sleepovers do not appear on the corresponding Solo de Chikas site, as that is not culturally accepted among Mexican-American families.

In addition to advertising that directs English-preferring Latina girls to the "Solo de Chikas" site, users visiting the U.S. general market site can click on the "Solo de Chikas" button along the left navigation bar. Girls from outside of the U.S. can choose which country they come from on the bottom navigation bar and experience localized ver-

---

Latino**Link**

Compare **BeingGirl.com,** Procter & Gamble's general market site for its Tampax and Always brands with **SoloDeChikas.com,** its site for English-speaking Latina girls.

sions of the branded content site, just as P&G rolled out country-specific sites for moms on Pampers Village.

Through this example, we see that it is not just the language that must be translated but the cultural context as well. When the average U.S. marketing manager thinks of "Hispanic" content online, he may first suggest simply translating the content into Spanish. This seems logical, but this example highlights how for second generation, English-preferring Hispanics, culturally customizing a website in English as Procter & Gamble has done with Solo de Chikas may provide a better option.

Google vs. Facebook: Two Approaches to Globalizing Websites

When multinationals launch a website in Spanish (or any "mega-language" spoken in more than one country), you must ask yourself whether it is better to launch individual, country-specific websites with unique domain names or whether it is better to launch one global website with a single ".com" domain name with different language settings and IP-targeted pages for each country. Let's compare how two global titans of the web—Google and Facebook—manage this issue by contrasting their two approaches. You can then discern which will be a better fit for your company and brands.

Early on, Google launched country-specific websites, each with its own unique domain name. Even users in the smallest-populated Latin American countries, like Panama, for example, have their own version of Google: Google.com.po. This allows Google to deliver country-specific search results and advertisements to users in each country. Its country-specific domain names also provide another benefit. For example, when Mexican-Americans want to find specific results from Mexico, they can always visit Google.com.mx from the United States instead of Google.com, the U.S. site. Try it for yourself. Search for the same term on Google.com. and Google.com.mx, and you will find different results. This, of course, begs the question, do ".com" sites signify U.S. sites, as in the case of Google, or global sites, like Facebook? At the same time, many American users may not even know that ".us" represents U.S. websites. We Americans have gotten spoiled being the center of the Internet for so long!

One of the challenges in launching country-specific URLs can be seen in the following graph. Visitors from Spain (in black) have actually been superseded by visitors from Latin America (in light grey) to Google's URL for Spain, Google.es, according to ComScore's multi-country media trend report (September 2008–September 2009).

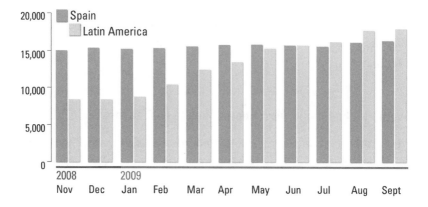

You may wonder why there are more Latin Americans than Spaniards visiting a site built for Spain. Following are a few reasons:

- Far more content is hosted on ".es" websites in Spain when compared with content in Latin America.

- When doing searches in Spanish on their in-country Google site, Latin Americans may find results on Google.es—for image searches or Google News, for example—without even noticing that they have arrived on the Google.es URL from their home country's Google site. Because the Google logo appears consistently in the upper left-hand corner, Latin American consumers may not notice any difference.

- Historically, Google Spain has offered more services (e.g., Google blog search in Spanish) than Google does in the emerging markets of Latin America because Spain's online advertising investment of US$1 billion dwarfs the combined total of all of the other Spanish-language, Latin American markets' online ad investments combined. Therefore, publishers in Spain, including Google, see much bigger incentives for developing tools and editorial products for Spain instead of for the emerging markets of Latin America, where investment is lacking.

- There are almost 92 million Latin Americans online (including Brazil) compared with about 20 million Spaniards online (ComScore, September 2009). Because there are far more Latin Americans online, those markets can collectively overshadow the entire Spanish market.

- Web browsers in Latin America may incorrectly default to Spanish from Spain as the default setting instead of Latin American Spanish, and so the embedded Google search box may default to Google.es.

- To a lesser extent, many Spaniards live in and travel to Latin America as employees of major Spanish corporation like Santander, BBVA, Telefonica, Inditex, and Havas, and probably use Google.es by default.

When multinationals offer better website features on one Spanish-language site in a more developed market, like Spain or the United States, and leave users in Latin America with sites that look like they are from 1999, Latin Americans online will quickly seek out better Spanish-language sites via search. Latin American users online prove just as sophisticated as users in the United States. This unfortunately can foster a separation between the "haves," in markets like the United States and Spain, from the "have nots" of Latin America.

One of the long-term drawbacks of rolling out "new" sites in big markets and maintaining "old" sites in others is that we essentially train users to cross borders to find better content. For example, one of IBM's usability consultants told me how, years ago, when IBM first launched a new, comprehensive site in Japanese, the users in Japan continued visiting the English-language site out of habit. After years of using the much more comprehensive English-language site, the Japanese had developed long-term habits of referring to it, and therefore trusted it more than the limited Japanese-language site.

Now, even though Google has taken on a country-specific approach to launching and customizing its websites and services, its mission statement remains "to organize the world's information and make it universally accessible and useful," which it clearly does extremely well.

In contrast to Google's approach, Facebook.com offers the entire world a consistent experience from just one URL. Users can select what language they prefer, whether it is Spanish, English, Portuguese, or even Pirate English, although certainly each country appears to have a primary default. While Google keeps its algorithm a secret (from spammers), Facebook "crowdsourced" the translations of its site, asking its users to translate its content and tools, as discussed in Chapter 7.

Facebook's global, language-specific approach works well in regions like Latin America that speak the same language (with the exception of Brazil), or countries like the United States that have large immigrant populations that speak a foreign language. It also works in countries like Switzerland that have three major languages: German, French, and Italian. The language-oriented, pan-regional view of the web, when compared with a country-specific one, fosters fast global growth of websites. Anyone who speaks Spanish, English, or the dozens of other languages Facebook offers can set up an account and use the site, no matter where he or she lives.

In reality, both Facebook and Google share far more in common behind the scenes than the differences in how they manage one ".com" address or the hundreds of URLs around the world, especially since both are media companies. Both target advertising by country (IP address) and by language. Both offer country-, language-, or user interest–specific content that is stored in users' preferences. Both manage large volumes of data with deep insights into what consumers want, need, and say, including response rates to advertising messages.

Arguing in favor of the Google approach, John Yunker, founder of the globalization consulting firm Byte Level and author of *Beyond Borders: Web Globalization Strategies*, recommends buying domain names in each country in which you do business for four reasons.

- **Trademark protection:** Would you want anyone else to own your brand name online?

- **Usability:** Just as Americans are predisposed to think ".com" when they first guess at a web address, so will other users outside the United States guess at their country code domains first.

- **Marketability:** In the end, you want your audience to think of your company as a local company.

- **Searchability:** Local search engines give preference to websites that use country-specific domain names. So, if you want to do well on Mexico's leading search engines, for example, it's best to invest in a .com.mx domain name.

A caution: Many countries like Argentina, Chile, and Colombia require that companies maintain a physical office within their borders in order to buy URLs with their respective country extensions.

You have to decide which model for managing URLs will work for your brand. If you sell an intangible service, like airplane tickets, music, or consulting, the Facebook, or global ".com," approach may work better for you, combined with country-specific landing pages customized to the local currency and language. On the other hand, if you offer country-specific information or sell physical products via distributors where the number and specifications of your product vary by country, then the Google approach may work better for you, because you can specify which products are available with specific distributors in each country. Neither one is right or wrong; it simply depends on your business requirements.

Localization and Globalization Checklist

In conclusion, as you seek to localize and globalize your website, think about the following four-step checklist from Yunker's consultancy (Byte Level Research). These steps can help ensure that your organization will steer its visitors to the best country- or language-specific websites that you have developed for them.

Preparation

- Assess your company's global readiness.
- Select your target markets and locales.
- Test your company and brand names, or create new names.
- Register country-specific domain names.
- Register internationalized domain names.
- Define the scope of your project, including the number of words and images requiring localization.
- Estimate and allocate your budget. Set the schedule.
- Solicit quotes from vendors.

Implementation

- Select your vendor.
- Prepare your source files such as text, graphics and scripts.
- Begin internationalization:
  - Currency conversion
  - Calendar and measurement (English versus metric system) conversions
  - Implement translation memory software.
- Build terminology glossary.
- Develop style guide.
- Begin localization:
  - Translation
  - Editing
  - Graphics and design
  - In-country review
  - Implement testing and Q&A processes (in-house and in-country).

Management

- Train in-country staff to support websites and customers:
  - Begin localization maintenance.
  - New source content must be localized.
- Changes to existing content must be reflected on all localized sites.
  - Support customers via all channels including phone, email and in-store.
  - Promote localized sites with advertising, PR and SEO/SEM initiatives.

Review

- Analyze sales by market.
  - Test your brand awareness.
  - Test the usability of your site.
  - Conduct quality audits of the translation(s).
  - Prepare for your next-generation website.

Lessons Learned

- Use localization best practices like global gateways, toggle buttons, geo-location and jump pages on your website to direct users to the appropriate, country-specific website.
- Stand in the shoes of the user and list the Spanish site as "Español."
- Remember that flags only represent countries, not languages.
- Culturally customize your website by considering the five value sets: individualism vs. collectivism, power distance, uncertainty avoidance, masculinity vs. femininity, and low vs. high context.
- Localize your website by following the four-step checklist: prepare, implement your plan, manage your efforts, and review the results.

You Can't Find Treasure Without a Map

By Pedro Mujica,
CEO, wecolab

Translated from Spanish by Joe Kutchera, as printed in *Yorokobu,* a Madrid-based marketing and design magazine, and used with permission.

These days, we all know and use online maps, the most well known of which is Google maps. Thanks to these online maps, we find the places and the directions for all of our day-to-day needs: trips, shopping, leisure activities, cultural events and so on. The advantages of using online maps are clear. We find directions to destinations, making sure we choose the shortest and quickest route, but we also discover new, interesting places along the way. They definitely make our lives easier because they help us save time and make better decisions. But there is always something more profound and powerful in a map because good maps always lead us to hidden treasure.

Where Is the Treasure?

The first generation of online maps focused on offering practical services with speed, utility and ease of use. The principal objective of this stage had been to provide maps that work, without interruptions, while improving search results. Mission accomplished. Nowadays, maps undergo continuous technological improvement, and millions use them every day. Their authentic value allows them to transform our lives and generate new business opportunities.

Interactive maps supply information about products and services from businesses but each time with more feedback from users. In this way, brands have begun to utilize maps to offer their products and services to consumers. In fact, some brands have already begun to find treasure: improved sales, new business units, etc. But this is just the beginning.

New Maps, New Treasures

We embark upon a new generation of interactive maps that allow us to create and explore new experiences with consumers—more emotional, more entertaining, and more useful. Maps have become a useful platform for winning and building customer loyalty as well as getting to know our customers. For example, look at what Google has done with "Local Business Center," its advertising service based on Google maps.

In the years ahead, we will see how maps evolve and become a more powerful communication and business channel. One of the best examples of this new era of online maps is Tokyo Fashion Map, which premiered at

the Cannes Festival in 2009 —an innovative ad campaign with 1,000 consumers passing along a parka coat to one another in a video above the map. The campaign introduced and promoted the new line of UNIQLO-branded parkas. It was so successful that they doubled their sales.

Source: Yorokobu, Tokyo Fashion Map http://www.uniqlo.com/uniqlo1000/

Also using this new approach of geo-marketing via online maps, Coca-Cola created a happiness map for "happing," its online community for young consumers. Members can search and demarcate their favorite places in the world on the "happing" map, sharing them with other community members. The campaign aimed to create a clear brand experience, build customer loyalty, and generate understanding about consumers.

Source: Yorokobu, www.CocaCola.es/happingmap

To develop an effective geo-marketing strategy, it is necessary to consider your target market, ROI objectives, key performance indicators, the technology plan, communication tactics, search engine optimization (SEO), search engine marketing (SEM) as well as development and maintenance of the map. In a world where we never lose our way because we always have a map of "our world" at hand on our computer or cell phone, the most important thing brands can do is translate their benefits and values into a personalized and relevant map for consumers. What isn't on a map doesn't exist. With geo-marketing, there are no secret maps with short cuts to hidden treasure. The strategy is the map. And only by beginning to explore can you begin to draw your own map and discover where the treasure is for your brand. Consumers use maps every day and already create their own. And your brand? Do you already have your treasure map?

Chapter 9

Targeting Latina Moms Online

IN THIS chapter, we will look at marketers and publishers who have effectively targeted one specific demographic online—Latina moms. In addition, we will analyze the growing overall trend of marketers developing informational, content-rich websites that attract consumers through helpful information or entertainment, historically, the domain of publishers.

The New Brand Marketing = Content Online

Latina moms are an incredibly important target market for reaching Latino families. As there are fewer content options for consumers who speak Spanish, producing content for Latinas presents an excellent opportunity to make a more authentic and lasting connection with them.

The major consumer packaged goods (CPG) marketers who have developed Spanish-language branded content for consumers include:

- Procter & Gamble: Pampers.com and BeingGirl.com
- Kraft Foods: ComidaKraft.com
- General Mills: Que Rica Vida
- Unilever: Vive Mejor
- SC Johnson: RightAtHome.com en español

Marketers and publishers choose to create unique content for a variety of reasons.

Building trust

Developing unique web content can educate consumers about a company's products or services in an inviting way, without a hard sell or interrupting them with a 30-second TV spot. It can improve customer satisfaction by answering shoppers' questions, and satisfy their needs by showing them how a product may solve a specific problem.

Virtual showrooms

Aggregate the knowledge of your best sales people and bring your product showroom to your website to answer questions from potential shoppers up front.

Moving up the consumer-consideration funnel

By providing culturally relevant content on their websites, marketers move their products closer to consumers' research and discovery phases, up the consumer-consideration funnel.

Owning information distribution

Whereas advertisers never thought of buying a TV or radio station in years past, today all brands must own and operate a website from which they can collect consumer feedback and insights. The almost nonexistent barriers to entry on the web invite everyone—advertisers, publishers, and agencies—to engage in direct and meaningful dialog with their customers. Easy starting points include starting a blog or launching a smart phone application.

Gaining access to concrete marketing data

Intangible brand value could never be measured before. Today, advertisers can measure exactly how much time each consumer spends on their sites and determine which features are the most popular. In essence, what used to exist in the mysterious ether of "marketing" now has become concrete through website analytics. No place is this clearer than in financial services, where websites become the welcome lobby and focus group for financial brands. H&R Block and American Family Insurance have significantly set themselves apart from the competition by helping consumers with useful, in-depth information in Spanish.

The magnetic force of search engine optimization (SEO)

Developing content for the web can attract consumers directly to your site so that you can tell your story the way you want it. Brands are only one search result, one click away from their target market, with a potential purchase or email sign-up.

Emotional connections

Make an emotional connection with users through stories and characters in three- to five-minute videos or even consumer-written blog posts that can be distributed across the web. Universally appealing stories can be shared on platforms like YouTube.

Branded Content Advertising Grows

According to a study by the Custom Publishing Council (CPC), total spending on branded content doubled in 2009 over 2008. This averages to about $1.8 million per company, with 51 percent spent on print publications (which most participants expect to decline in 2010), 27 percent on Internet media, and 22 percent on categories such as video or audio, which were measured for the first time this year. Lori Rosen, executive director of the CPC, says, "78 percent of respondents reported that branded content is more effective than advertising."

Launching Web Content Initiatives Globally: Pampers Village

At the Interactive Advertising Bureau (IAB) Spain's annual conference, Eleonore Ogrinz, Procter & Gamble's associate director of media and communications for Western Europe, explained how the digital medium enables Procter & Gamble to accomplish three main marketing goals: serve new consumers, create engaging customer experiences, and facilitate greater listening to its customers.

According to Ogrinz, the marketing process starts with the consumer. When looking through the digital lens, Procter & Gamble asks questions, listens to consumers' responses and observes consumer behavior. Procter & Gamble obviously understands the global nature of the web as it rolls out brand content initiatives on a global basis. (See the Tampax/Always example in Chapter 8 and Pampers example later in this chapter.) While one targets teen girls and the other targets pregnant women, both focus on answering questions and assuaging concerns as they go through major life stage changes like puberty and pregnancy.

Ogrinz emphasized that creativity is enormously important at Procter & Gamble, and that the simplicity of an idea can reflect its true creative brilliance. "It's all about the content," she said, showing the baby-naming tool on Pampers Village (Pampers.com) that creates a long-term relationship with moms via its eCRM data-collection platform.

LatinoLink

Procter & Gamble's U.S. Latino site **es.pampers.com**

The site structure reflects both the company's desire for simplicity and its emphasis on content. The site navigation on the U.S. Hispanic site features five channels—pregnancy, new baby, baby, toddler, and preschooler—plus a channel for "Me,"

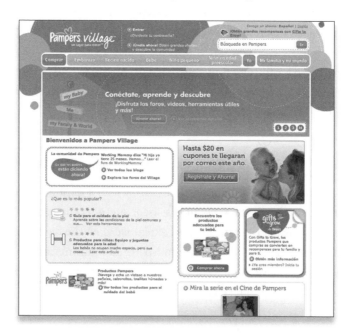

the mom, and "My Family, My World." Delving into each channel, beyond the simple and clean site navigation, articles can be found by category (e.g., feeding, development, sleep), content type (blog, forum, play & learn), or keyword. Both sites stay true to their brand identity with the same color scheme, navigation, and tagline in Spanish (*un hogar para crecer*, or "a home for growing").

Most importantly, the company rolled out the initiative on a global basis. Developing content for one Spanish-language market and leaving another one with an anemic site does not work on the web, so the two Spanish-language sites were launched simultaneously. At the same time, each site features cultural customizations. For example, the U.S. Hispanic site shows the "Pampers Village" brand whereas the Mexican site reads "Comunidad Pampers." Below the main "Cruisers" product information call-out, the U.S. Hispanic site highlights the "Pampers Community" with blogs and forums, online shopping ("Buy now"), and local promotions ("Gifts to Grow") in the lower right-hand corner. The Mexican site features "build your own blog" and the baby-naming tool in the main content promotion box plus the new articles, newsletters, and product info promotional boxes from left to right. Procter & Gamble aims to educate consumers and provide helpful information to them.

Babies Beyond Borders

BabyCenter.com, like Pampers Village, provides moms online with information about conception, pregnancy, birth, and early childhood. As the leading site in the category, BabyCenter leads moms (and dads) through each stage of their pregnancy and the first three years of their children's lives via a free email newsletter with week-by-week updates on what to expect. Launched in 1997, the site was purchased by Johnson & Johnson in 2001. Because pregnant moms provide their expected due date when they sign up for the newsletter, BabyCenter can access real-time data about when women get pregnant, where they are in the pregnancy process, and, most importantly, what's on their minds (by looking at what they search for).

BabyCenter launched BabyCenter en Español, its first Spanish-language site targeting U.S. Hispanics in 2007 because so many advertisers requested a platform for reaching Hispanic moms online, according to Jon Stross, the site's vice president of international and U.S. Hispanic. While many U.S. Hispanics embraced the helpful information on the site, BabyCenter discovered that many Latin Americans and even Spaniards discovered and used the site soon after its debut. So, BabyCenter Spain came to life in 2008, and its Mexico sibling followed in 2009. Even after launching these country-specific sites for the largest Spanish-language markets, all three Spanish-language sites each find that a majority of their visitors come from outside of their "home" country. Today, the U.S. Hispanic site reaches 700,000 unique visitors each month (September 2009), according to ComScore, with 24 percent coming from the United States, 66 percent coming from Latin America, and 10 percent from Spain. The company reports that more than 300,000 women from across the Spanish-language world have signed up for its newsletter.

Stross calls BabyCenter an "insights engine," which aggregates users' feedback via comments in community areas, emails, surveys, panels, search statistics, content use, and focus groups. In addition, BabyCenter often receives requests from Latin Americans to have its retail partners (e.g., Diapers.com) offer shipping throughout the region. As you can see from the following comments, moms truly appreciate the information and support that BabyCenter provides in Spanish, especially for questions that they may not feel comfortable asking their doctors:

"I am 19 weeks pregnant and I subscribed to the English site at 8 weeks. A few weeks ago I switched to the Spanish site and I like it more because you really take into account the Latino perspective," says Faride.

"I am alone and my family is far away and I don't have anybody I can talk to about my symptoms. Thanks to you, now I am well informed. You are my new family!" says Adriana.

About the article on postpartum depression, Karla says, "What timely and great information, just when I needed it! I have suffered depression for 6 years and it is very helpful for me to know the risks

I might incur during and after pregnancy. Thank you BabyCenter, for informing us in such a meaningful way!"

Luz says, "My baby is 7 months old, and I didn't understand that at this stage babies suffer separation anxiety and want to be with you all the time, and that's why sometimes he doesn't want me to leave him alone even to go the bathroom. Before I read the information in the site, I thought he was sick or acting up. Phew! I feel so relieved to have you in my life."

Because culture and vocabulary in the Spanish-speaking world are so varied, BabyCenter en Español uses a universal, neutral Spanish and localizes details from different countries-of-origin. For example, BabyCenter compares the amount of caffeine in a Cuban cup of coffee versus Argentinean mate, analyzes the higher rate of itchy skin problems in pregnant women of Chilean origin or gallbladder stones in women of Mexican origin, and showcases family recipes from several Latin American countries.

The editorial team at BabyCenter's San Francisco headquarters manages the U.S. Hispanic content and oversees the international editors, writers, and medical advisory boards in each local market. The local teams translate, adapt, and customize about 150 articles per year from the U.S. site for local markets. This includes localizing already-existing articles as well as adding unique content for each market. BabyCenter currently has 21 unique sites, including those dedicated to U.S. Hispanics, Mexico, Spain, and Brazil. "Even in countries where we haven't yet localized, moms still find value in the content we've written for the U.S. Hispanic audience as so many elements of this life stage are universal," Stross says.

As BabyCenter researched which country to use as its main hub for Spanish speakers, it found through user feedback that a site focused on U.S. health practices would generally be more trusted across the region than one focused on Mexico or Spain because the United States has a reputation for providing high-quality and constantly updated medical research and health recommendations. This, of course, builds trust among online readers. In contrast, many Latin American countries have uneven health systems when comparing rural or urban hospitals. Often, the public or

even the doctors cannot easily obtain the latest research or recommendations. "My experience when visiting Mexico's hospitals and doctors, for
instance, is that the doctors themselves research the latest information
and recommendations provided by the American Academy of Pediatrics
(AAP), the Centers for Disease Control (CDC), and other American medical
institutions," says Isidra Mencos, the editor of BabyCenter en Español.

Across the Spanish-language world, moms' main concerns and
dreams are universal: they want to have a healthy pregnancy and baby.
As such, mom and pregnancy sites see a lot of traffic from around the
world. Some of the specific health issues and concerns, that BabyCenter
addresses include:

- Breastfeeding: "I don't have enough milk!"
- Solid feeding: "My child doesn't eat enough!"
- Ingrained habits like complementing breast milk with formula very
  early on
- Tuberculosis during pregnancy due to a lack of vaccinations in
  Latin America
- Help for recent arrivals in understanding the U.S. health care
  system
- How to deal with cultural differences if your doctor is not Hispanic
- When it is best to pierce a baby girl's ears for earrings
- How to deal with the deluge of visitors after the birth of a baby

BabyCenter also answers questions about pregnancy myths and traditional medical practices among Hispanics, one of the most popular sections, where it covers issues like:

- Mayan massage for conception
- Safety of traditional healer practices
- A coin on the belly button will make an innie"

For English-preferring Hispanics, BabyCenter also provides a "Latino
Moms" community on the English-language site where women can find
other moms who share the same due date or country-of-origin.

All Things Baby: Global from the Start

Todobebé, based in Miami, has been "global from the start," according to the company's COO, Cynthia Nelson. Like BabyCenter, Todobebé provides expert advice to millions of Spanish-speaking moms through its digital community and content websites. Unlike BabyCenter, which has three different URLs for U.S. Hispanic, Spain, and Mexico audiences, Todobebé offers content on only one global ".com" site, which, according to ComScore (September 2009), sees 52 percent of its visitors from Latin America, 32 percent from the United States, and 17 percent from Spain (more than 100 percent due to rounding).

"All Things Baby," as its name means in Spanish, develops its multiplatform, evergreen content in its Miami headquarters using a universal Spanish. Nelson says, "We take great care to ensure that we don't use regional words or slang in our content. In this way, we reach everyone with the same, clear information. If your baby is crying at night, you can be a CEO or a taxi cab driver and you want information about how to get them to sleep. That is why we have built a global business model: A mom is a mom is a mom. She wants the best for her kids whether she is in the U.S., Mexico, or Bombay, Russia, or China."

The company's social network, Mi Todobebé, provides a platform where moms can speak directly with, connect to, and listen to other moms. "It's the number one feature on the site. Social interaction and peer-to-peer communication with consumers is the backbone of Todobebe.com. It is the baseline for content creation, research, and knowledge about our growing consumer audience," says Nelson.

Culturally Relevant Content from General Mills

Imagine moving to China and taking your first trip to the grocery store to buy food. What do these packages say? How can I find the ingredients that I want to make the food that I know? Which brand is best? The bottom line: What do you recognize in the store? Nothing! It's all in Chinese.

Ursula Mejia-Melgar, the multicultural marketing manager at General Mills, makes that analogy when she describes what her target audience—Spanish-dominant Latina moms—experiences when they go to the store for the first time in the United States. Que Rica Vida, General Mills' Spanish-language website, aims to serve its audience as a trusted friend and resource by providing culturally relevant content that can help moms adjust to their new lives in America. The site aims to empower Latina moms by providing them with information about raising their children, tending to their illnesses and preventing them, making sure they don't fall behind in school and cooking for their families. The section on recipes and ingredients provides tips and tools about how to be a better shopper. And General Mills works with content partners like Dr. Aliza, for example, who offer health advice to consumers who visit the site. In addition to its

*Latino**Link***

QueRicaVida.com

website, General Mills also distributes 400,000 audited copies of a quarterly magazine under the same name—*Que Rica Vida.*

General Mills produces content in Spanish because Spanish-dominant Latina moms have different needs, wants, desires, and family values, and a company's marketing materials ought to reflect that.

Buying Your Way into the Content Marketplace

What happens when marketers buy content companies, as Johnson & Johnson did with BabyCenter, compared with marketers' content sites such as Comida Kraft or Unilever's Vive Mejor? The two models are quite different. **Jon Stross,** BabyCenter's vice president of U.S. Hispanic and international sales, says BabyCenter operates as a separate media company, and the majority of revenues come from non–Johnson & Johnson brands, many of which are competitors. While BabyCenter aims to sell advertising, there are no products or brand mentions within the articles. Comida Kraft, on the other hand, clearly promotes and encourages use of Kraft's products in the recipes offered on the site.

Cynthia Nelson, the COO of TodoBebé, does not see a threat from marketers producing content. These branded sites can complement her site's content, in her case, with parenting information. "We partner all the time with these large players. It's taken us more than 10 years and millions of dollars [to build our media business]. They are not going to ever spend the time, money, or resources to get there. It isn't a model that any large CPG would undertake. We have millions of users and thousands of articles, videos, access to over 200 TV shows, radio programs, and games," says Nelson, who emphasizes that the best thing to do is focus on who you are to the consumer and what you do best.

The entry of marketers into the content business is not limited to the United States. Two major marketers in the Spanish-language world, Telefonica (the phone company based in Spain) and France Telecom, own Terra and Starmedia, respectively. Like Johnson & Johnson, both portals operate apart from their parent companies.

It appears that the blending of marketers and content media will cause the landscape to change as we move further into the 21st century. Most telling is Amazon's acquisition of Digital Photography Review (dpreview.com), the web's most comprehensive site for digital camera reviews in English, as reported by *Business Wire* (May 14, 2007). The Digital Photography Review content builds trust for the customer and brings Amazon further up the consideration funnel where its forums provide deeper insights to Amazon about what consumers look for when searching for the camera that's right for them.

Lessons Learned

- By developing websites with more robust content, brand marketers can build trust with consumers, move up the consumer-consideration funnel, collect customer data, gain consumer insights online, and attract consumers through online content and SEO. This significantly improves the way they engage with and listen to consumers.
- The digital medium enables companies like Procter & Gamble to accomplish marketing goals such as serving new consumers,

creating engaging consumer experiences, and facilitating greater consumer listening.

- Content sites act as insight engines into what consumers' information needs are by hour, day of the week, month, and season. This can yield a much deeper understanding of consumer behavior via website analytics and feedback.

- Marketers invest in branded content initiatives because they can be more effective than other forms of marketing and can better educate and retain customers.

- It is wise to launch Spanish-language sites—U.S. Hispanic in addition to Mexican and Latin American sites—in tandem across the worldwide web, as Procter & Gamble did with its Pampers' site so that web searchers from each Spanish-language country are directed to the appropriate site.

- Universal experiences like having a baby or being a mom work well on forums, as readers greatly value sharing experiences and information.

- The United States has a reputation for high-quality medical research and trustworthy health information, which is easily found online. So users from around the world will visit our sites, in Spanish or English, for that reason.

Ford: Tu Voz en Tu Vida

By Dave Rodriguez
Multicultural Marketing Manager
Ford Motor Company and
Maylinn De La Maza,
Account Director
Zubi

LatinoLink
TuVozEnTuVida.com

Background

From previously conducted research, Ford Motor Company identified Hispanic women as an influential consumer market in the United States due to their position as heads of household and decision makers within their families. With that in mind, Ford partnered with Time Inc. Content Solutions to identify the content gaps that existed in current online women's sites. The findings revealed there was a need for quality content that could speak directly to Hispanic women about the themes of empowerment. Furthermore, the best area within Time Warner (at that time) to speak to Ford's target market was AOL Latino's women's site, Tu Vida.

Connecting with the Target Audience

Ford, together with AOL and Zubi, launched its "Tu Voz en Tu Vida" site in May 2009 to target U.S. Hispanic women. Using the tagline "un sitio de Latinas para Latinas," or "a site for Latinas by Latinas," the site connects with the user through the unique insight that Hispanic women who embrace their Latin culture, regardless of their level of assimilation, are caught in a bicultural struggle that general market counterparts do not face. Whether due to language barriers, cultural nuances, or taboos, Hispanic women have specific needs and interests in varied life stages and seek information that speaks directly to their concerns. Who better to provide those insights than other Latinas?

Content Development

There is a new breed of Latina emerging in the United States. These Latinas feel more empowered to manage a busy lifestyle and seek self-development. They want to take better care of themselves, become more organized, improve their finances, advance their education or careers, and balance work and family. The four Tu Voz coaches each stand out as experts in their respective areas of expertise. And as Latinas who live in the United States, they not only bring credibility but also add a cultural texture to these areas of expertise.

The five channels on the site include:

- Bienestar, or "Well-being," featuring Dr. Aliza Lifshitz
- Vive mas, or "Better living," featuring Maria Marin
- Éxito, or "Success," featuring Mariela Dabbah
- Finanzas, or "Finances," featuring Maria I. Ferre
- Al volante, or "At the steering wheel," featuring . . . the car!

AOL Latino has the most popular women's channel, and we wanted to capitalize on that existing traffic. Additionally, AOL Latino has proven to be an excellent partner to Ford in previous projects where developing and promoting custom content was required.

Localizing the Site and "Flavor" of Spanish

We strive to "localize" our site by providing content that is relevant to U.S. Hispanic women's concerns, habits, characteristics and styles of life. In addition, we cover information that may be of interest to a particular community of U.S. Hispanic women via the diffusion of conferences, seminars, and other resources of interest in their local community.

The Spanish we use on the site can be considered "modern" from a stylistic and content viewpoint, yet "formal" from a grammatical one. The site serves Latinas nationwide, so we try to limit the use of dialects or regional variations of Spanish; instead, we try to maintain the "flavor" of the Spanish used in Tu Voz a bit more standard.

Success Metrics

These range from overall visits and engagement within the site to Ford digital advertising performance to a study indicating brand favorability and opinion among Tu Voz users. Our visitors gave high ratings for the site's content and the range of information available. The "bienestar" and "vive mas" channels seem to be the most popular among our visitors.

Ford's partnership in this initiative has resulted in positive opinion and increased consideration of Ford's vehicles. Because of Ford's global brand awareness, some international visitors found the site. While 66% of Tu Voz's visitors came from the United States, 25 percent visited from Mexico, and the remaining 9% encompass Latin America countries.

Advice for Launching Spanish-Language Sites

- Don't offer a straight translation from an English-language site
- Take into account ties to countries-of-origin
- Make it relevant—experience of living in the United States has to be reflected in content

Chapter 10

Reaching Latinos with Content

THE SPANISH writer Miguel de Cervantes famously said, "Tell me thy company, and I'll tell thee what thou art." In this chapter, I will outline how to surround yourself with the best business partners in content development as well as online media, specifically comparing online publishers and ad networks. In addition, I will highlight how to establish systems to distribute content on social networks and optimize your Spanish-language sites for search.

Evaluating Content Partners

You may ask, why work with a content partner or publisher/media company like Univision, BabyCenter or AOL Latino? Whether you choose to translate content from English or work with a publisher to create new, original content, focus on hiring content partners that can deliver the highest quality and reach.

In the case of Ford, AOL Latino provided access to a pool of professional writers, designers, editors and usability experts as well as a built-in distribution channel, AOL Latino, to promote its new branded website. In addition, Ford bought media to drive traffic to Tu Voz en Tu Vida. This partnership delivered both high-quality editorial and built-in reach. In the case of a translation company, select a partner that can help you with the translation, hosting, analytics and/or search engine optimization for your website content. While translation companies do not have built-in reach as companies like AOL Latino can provide, delivering recommendations about or managing search engine optimization or marketing can make the difference between making your website a success or failure. Also, ask how each translation company can help manage machine translation services (e.g., Google Translate) of user-generated product reviews and community content areas as this will grow in importance in the years ahead.

When considering content partners, figure out what type of content your target market wants most and that will often lead you to the appropriate partner. Some questions to ask during the evaluation process include:

- What type of content does your target audience consume?
  - Telenovelas?
  - How-to content?
  - Games?
  - Country-of-origin news?
- What age is your target audience and how much do they consume content across platforms or multitask while watching television?
- Which digital media appeals the most to your audience?
  - Video?
  - Text?
  - Mobile?
- How much interactivity do your users seek? (Very little among TV watchers or a lot among young mobile users)

If your audience consumes a lot of country-of-origin content, you might work with publishers like Televisa, Medio Tiempo, or the leading newspapers or newspaper groups in Latin America (GDA or PAL) to develop custom microsites.

If you want to reach early adopters, work with some of the mobile companies to develop branded applications for you.

If your target audience prefers watching telenovelas, work with Univision or Telemundo to put together a branded site featuring the latest clips or episode summaries. Or, maybe your company wants to work with a media company that has a content production facility to develop custom videos.

In interviewing marketers for this book, many executives admitted how easy it is to overestimate the cost and time involved in choosing and working with a content development partner. If you choose five sites, that requires five times the cost and time. Therefore, many recommended working with only one content development partner in order to simplify the process.

One of the main reasons why marketers choose to develop web content is to further optimize their website for search and boost rankings for the specific keywords that relate to their products. While it may seem easy to some marketers, many media and content companies find that advertisers often overlook the fact that their very content providers, the media companies, become their competitive set online and instead only look at the other brands in their category trying to do the same thing.

Distributing Content on Social Platforms

Once you develop content in Spanish on your websites, you need to consider how you will distribute it. While much of the online content you develop today lives on websites, in the future it will be distributed to wherever users go: social networks, within banner ads, search, mobile applications, and whatever new platforms evolve going forward. You can host videos on YouTube, and then run those same videos on your own website, on media sites within banners, or as part of content integration packages, as well as allowing bloggers to syndicate it across their own sites. Ideally consumers can access content any time of the day, wherever they want to, and on any platform.

As your messages spread across the web, controlling your message becomes more complicated and the context in which consumers receive your message can make a big difference.

Setting Up Content Delivery Systems

We can learn from one of the major movie studios about how it set up its online content distribution and localization system and how it shares content between its Latin American and U.S. Hispanic teams. This story highlights how other marketers can set up their own content distribution systems pan-regionally or for multiple sites. It also forecasts what will evolve in the world of social media. Marketers need ways to quickly distribute their messages and creative onto their own websites and across social networks today and in the years ahead.

This film studio, which preferred to remain nameless, develops its film websites centrally in Los Angeles and then uses an automated website builder to distribute, customize, and localize its website content for each site across Latin America and the world. The studio created the user interface for its automated website builder to facilitate the "localization" of film sites into several languages. Its agencies and local offices receive alerts when files appear in the system. Local marketing managers can upload the trailers as well as the logo of a film in their local language. Next, the translated text appears in the appropriate fields, and the managers click "publish now" to have it appear on their country-specific websites. Although most content is reused globally, the studios are aware that some content is country specific; for example films released in the U.S. have English subtitles for the U.S. Hispanic market and Spanish subtitles for the Latin American markets.

Its agency in Bogota, Colombia, supports all of its regional offices as they adapt the film sites using the automated website builder and translate advertising to local tastes. Together, they always try to do the work once, so the local offices do not incur any extra expenses. This includes localizing banners and search ads for each market. In addition, the agency receives online media plans and adapts the online pieces received from headquarters to local specifications—with the exception of Argentina and Mexico—where campaigns are managed separately. Video materials are adapted to Spanish internally in L.A. while games and social media applications are adapted by the agency in Colombia. When the studio measures return on investment, it analyzes statistics such as number of content downloads, time spent watching a video, and unique registrations for contests or games.

In summary, this studio recommends following these tips for launching and localizing a Spanish-language site:

- Use universal Spanish for cost efficiency.
- Develop localized content to create a connection with consumers.

- Syndicate content through social media.

- Mistakes can actually help you learn and improve your campaigns and processes while building relationships with end consumers.

Using Ad Networks to Target Hispanics Online

Now that we have defined how to evaluate and choose content partners, this section will outline how to deliver audiences to your websites through your media partners using a variety of targeting techniques. The consumer behavior of cross-border media consumption requires a new mechanism for buying and selling media: online advertising networks. Because of this trend, a number of ad networks have opened up shop to serve the needs of advertisers trying to reach both Hispanics visiting foreign websites and Spanish speakers abroad visiting U.S. websites.

Benefits of Ad Networks and Premium Sites

Premium publishers, like Univision.com, Terra.com, and Batanga.com, sell their banner or search advertising directly to marketers or advertising agencies, just as television, magazine, and outdoor media companies have done for years. In contrast, online advertising networks separate the two core competencies of media companies, ad sales and editorial development, by representing just the advertising space and letting publishers manage their own content development. Ad networks use online ad servers to represent hundreds or thousands of websites directly or in many cases on a blind basis, where they sell banner space based upon the type of website or content on the page. Ad networks essentially arbitrage banner-advertising space, buying impressions, or ads viewed, for a low, cost per thousand (CPM) and selling at a higher one.

Ad networks add value to banner advertising by aggregating online ad space so that marketers can quickly reach large numbers of people across a variety of websites and also by offering a variety of targeting tools, which usually yields more relevant advertising to users and better click-throughs to advertisers.

Marketers can choose to promote their own messages on premium websites or through ad networks. Usually a media plan includes both types. There are advantages and disadvantages to both approaches.

Some of the advantages of working with online advertising networks include lower CPMs, greater reach for big campaigns, the capability of quickly and efficiently optimizing campaigns, country-of-origin targeting, aggregating specialized ad inventory in mobile and video, as well as behavioral and contextual targeting for targeting bilinguals.

The benefits of working with premium sites include greater control of where your ad runs, content integration going beyond display advertising, sponsorship opportunities, and integration with emerging media such as mobile and video.

The main drawback of working with ad networks is limited transparency (depending on the reporting of the ad network). Ideally, you want to ask for contextual and behavioral reports as well as reports by site. "Being transparent allows advertisers to know exactly where their ads are running, at all times," says Marta Martinez, the CEO of StarMedia, which promotes itself as a completely transparent network.

In the case of premium sites, the drawbacks include higher CPMs and limited inventory, as very few Hispanic sites reach more than 20 percent of the Hispanic audience online. In addition, it's harder to scale with individual sites because of the challenges in dealing with multiple points of contact with the different publishers or media companies.

In the years ahead, Christopher Stanley, CEO and founder of Alcance Media Group, foresees marketers looking for specific country-of-origin targeting. "I see an increase in the number of sites for specific countries such as Cuba or Venezuela that are being operated from the U.S," he says.

Comparing Hispanic Ad Networks: A Formula

The table on the following page lists Spanish-language ad networks and their features. Though this data is likely to change, you can use this as a template for comparing Hispanic ad networks in the future. See below for the descriptions of the different types of targeting. This list features the Hispanic-only ad networks. In addition, you can consider the larger online media companies like AOL, Yahoo! and Audience Science, all of which sell Hispanic online media as part of their offerings.

Hispanic Ad Networks

	Number of Sites	Unique Visitors (million)	Content Sponsorships	Geographic Targeting	Contextual Targeting	Country-of-Origin	Behavioral Targeting	Browser, OS, or Language	Additional Services
Alcance	125 sites, including: Mundo Sin Barreras HOY Café Magazine Havana Journal CIU San Francisco Azteca El Nuevo Herald Diario de America	8.3 (server)	X	X	X	X	X	X	Custom publisher recruitment, web design, outsourced ad operations for small/ mid-size agencies
Batanga	312 sites, including: Hispano • Clarin.com ElSalvador.com Batanga LaNacion.com.ar El Colombiano Cromos.com.co elheraldo.hn ElUniversal.com.co LaRepublica.pe LaVerdad.com	14 (Com-Score)	X	X	X	X	X	X	Banner solutions such as in-banner videos, page push down and crawler units
EZ-Target (Terra)	100+ sites, including: AS.com • El Pais Goal.com • CincoDias.com Daddy Yankee • Hola.com GolTV.tv • Venevision.net MissVenezuela.com	9.5 (Com-Score)	X	X	X	X	X	X	Mobile development and ad serving solutions for publishers
Hola Networks	450+ sites including Azteca America portals as well as Spanish Broadcasting System sites	13.3 (Com-score)	X	X		X	X	X	
Orange/ StarMedia	20+ sites, including: starMedia • El Mundo Marca • Spil Games The Weather Channel en Español	2 (Com-Score)	X	X		Only for email marketing	X		Development of branded entertainment
Univision	64 sites, including: Caracol TV • Revista Caras Perfil.com • El Espectador TyC Sports Ambito Financiero	2 (Quant-cast)	X	X	X	X	X		

Targeting Technologies Online

The most successful campaigns are those that combine the right mix of tools to properly segment and reach a specific target within the right context. Not only should your messages be culturally relevant, but so should the environments in which they are placed. Following are some targeting techniques to consider.

Geo-Targeting

Geo-targeting (also known as IP targeting) to specific countries, states, or DMAs is popular in segmenting Hispanics from different countries of origin or marketing to specific countries across Latin America. Kristina Canada, Media Director at Media 8, says "We focus on aggressive IP targeting to reach our desired audiences. This strategy can come into play when reaching U.S. Hispanics via U.S. IP targeting on best-in-class Latin American Spanish language sites. Or, we use it in reaching key Latin American audiences via IP targeting on U.S. Spanish language sites that have substantial traffic coming from Latin America."

An important tip to remember is to request that your online media vendors deliver ad impressions in the U.S. only. "For a long time, publishers in the U.S. have cheated advertisers. Advertisers with U.S. campaigns don't want Latin American consumers seeing their ads; it's wasted impressions. Yet U.S. publishers continue to run international traffic against local campaigns," says Cameron Yuill, CEO of Adgent 007, an international online ad rep firm that represents U.S. publishers outside of the U.S. and international publishers within the U.S. "Some of the most well-known publishers in the U.S. are the biggest offenders. It's geo-fraud and it has to stop. It's really a win/win/win if the industry calls a halt to this practice: advertisers get only the impressions they want; publishers get better results for the campaigns they run so advertisers are happier and consumers in Latin America see ads relevant to them, not U.S. ads."

Behavioral Targeting

Yahoo! and other ad networks and publishers can behaviorally target Hispanics online by identifying users that read Spanish-language pages online, which can then be used as a basis for building behavioral consumer profiles (with information saved in cookies). Publishers make assumptions about users' surfing habits targeting them as "Spanish-language cultural enthusiasts," who visit Spanish-language pages within an ad network, "Moms," who visit content areas targeting mothers, or "New car shoppers," who visit pages about cars.

"Online behavior allows publishers to more accurately target users on Yahoo! rather than relying on content to target users (like magazine and television media) we can target users based upon their behavior and find them wherever and whenever they are on Yahoo!," says Chris Emme of Yahoo! en español.

Behavioral targeting can provide effective results for marketers who want to reach a large number of online consumers while aggregating consumer ad response data and optimizing results. Gail Galuppo, CMO of Western Union says, "Behavioral targeting is our most successful strategy for reaching online Hispanic consumers. We also use broad-reach and niche, country-of-origin news, video and sports sites to reach consumers who are likely to send money home."

Spanish-Language Browser Targeting

Some marketers use more advanced approaches within ad networks such as Spanish-language browser targeting, in order to reach Spanish-dominant users that default their Internet browsers to their native language. Kristina Canada of Media 8 found that these users make up about 15 percent of the U.S. Hispanic online population.

Country-of-Origin Targeting

Some online ad networks can aggregate U.S. ad impressions from Mexican websites. For example, if an airline wants to reach consumers interested in flying to Mexico for the holidays, it can target an audience that regularly reads news from Mexico.

Contextual Targeting

This type of targeting enables clients to place banner or text ads alongside relevant content. Marla Skiko, SVP at SMG Multicultural says, "We use contextual targeting to seek Moms in cooking, family, and entertaining content across a variety of sites and channels. Where applicable, we created a behavioral segmentation for 'avid Latina chefs' to reach those moms who really enjoy cooking and prepare more than an average number of meals per week at home to more closely match our message with our core intended user. Based on the performance of the behaviorally targeted placements, we created behavioral segmentations for several other clients as we see much better results when the message matches the media environment."

Content Category Targeting

Just as marketers buy media in specific magazine categories or brands, they can also buy online media across specific content sites or types. As an example, Kingston Technology targeted users based on site type. It purchased media on computer sites (for its flash drives), music sites (for its micro cards), and on Universia.net, a site aimed squarely at university students who needed the transportability of flash drives.

Social Media Profile Targeting

In addition to creating a fan page for your product or brand and inviting customers to interact with you on it, you can also purchase advertising on social media sites. Social networks can target advertising based on registered users' age, sex, hometown, interests, favorite music or movies, and even the employer or industry in which they work when users have listed that information in their profiles. This can ensure that you deliver your message with nearly 100 percent certainty to your desired demographic. Nevertheless, many advertisers ask how effective advertising is on social networks. That will be determined by how you contextually develop and integrate content into each specific social network. In addition, it will also depend upon how social networks contextually promote your content, games, or tools within the stream of user updates.

Creative Re-Targeting

As an extension of behavioral targeting, this type of targeting tracks users who have been served an ad, typically on an ad network. That user is then retargeted with the same creative messaging as he travels across sites on the ad network. Essentially it "follows" users based upon their proven media consumption habits, thereby delivering a more relevant advertisement.

Privacy Matters

While the above-mentioned technologies can drive precise results for clients, it also begs the question of how they affect consumer privacy. The Interactive Advertising Bureau encourages online media companies to follow its privacy principles so as to meet consumers' privacy expectations and create a viable marketing ecosystem. You can visit www.IAB.net/privacymatters to learn more about its recommendations for consumer data and privacy.

Less (Content) Is More (Unless You Have Nothing in Spanish)

It behooves marketers to follow Mies van der Rohe's advice, "less is more." He stripped away the decorative elements of his architectural design to create his signature minimalistic buildings. In her book *Content Strategy for the Web*, Kristina Halvorson points out that content requires a great deal of time, money, energy, and persuasion of the powers-that-be, and also that users will never magically generate content for you. So, the less you have, the less you will have to manage going forward and the less content that consumers will have to sift through to get what they want.

How Much Choice Do Consumers Want?

In an *eMarketer* report titled "How Much Choice Do Consumers Want?" (March, 2008), several analysts discussed whether consumers want more or fewer choices when shopping. "It's part of why manufacturers and service providers put so much information online for consumers. Yet researchers at the University of Iowa found that people who have only a little information about a product are happier with that product than people who have more information."

This highlights how important it is to be selective when you publish content online and carefully maintain the information you have. At the same time, from a usability perspective, you can provide links for consumers who need more detailed information on separate, additional pages.

This is where recommendations from peers can be especially powerful as analyst Jeffrey Grau explains. "One of the touted benefits of peer recommendations, such as those offered on social shopping sites, is that they help simplify consumer decision making. The Internet is a rich source of information for learning about products, comparing them and finding where they can be purchased." Consumers like it when they are told what to buy by friends, a search engine, or colleagues on a social network.

Analyst Debra Aho Williamson's personal story encapsulates the less-is-more mantra very well, "When I was getting ready for our wedding, I went with my husband to the caterer to choose a wedding cake. The caterer told me, 'You can have anything you want, any flavor, any filling, any design.' It was too much for me and I had a legendary breakdown right there in the caterer's office (my husband still tells the story, 14 years later). The next day the caterer called and suggested three options. I chose one and the cake was amazing. Lesson learned: Given a few choices, I felt great and still empowered. Given infinite choice, I was paralyzed and fearful."

Search Engine Optimization and Paid Search

In addition to the targeting techniques above for banner advertising, search engines provide a key platform for getting the word out. Here, we will compare the differences between search engine optimization (SEO) and paid search, or search engine marketing.

Take a look at the results on any search query and you will see the "sponsored links" on Google, "sponsored results" on Yahoo! and "sponsored sites" on Bing along side and above the unpaid, "natural," or "organic," search results in the middle of the web page. You could compare the paid results to advertising in a magazine and the natural results to the articles or content.

Advertisers buy their paid search results on a cost-per-click (CPC) basis via auction-based systems. The highest CPC bid for a search term will appear at the top of the page. As you scroll down, advertisers with lower

CPC bids will appear further down the page. In addition, search engines typically "reward" ads that are better written and receive better clicks, as these ads both yield more revenue for the search engines and provide more relevant results for users. You can say that paid search has developed into a science as CPC ad buyers and sellers can analyze spreadsheets of data for thousands of keyword terms and their corresponding click through and sales conversion results.

In contrast, search engine optimization (SEO) could be called an art as it is a bit murkier and more complicated but incredibly valuable nonetheless.

It seems obvious to state, but the higher up a site appears in the natural search results, the more likely users will click on it. What makes SEO complicated is that the search engines do not divulge their algorithms and therefore, SEO experts mostly make educated guesses, albeit sometimes very good ones, at how it works. SEO can be applied to different types of search such as image search, local search, or video search.

"Even when they seem like two ways of getting to the same place, search engine optimization (SEO) and paid search are fairly different disciplines at their core. SEO is a tactic that needs to combine code optimizations with a good deal of ongoing public relations and good copywriting," says Jonatan Zinger, the director of Search Marketing at Media 8.

When clients hope to drive direct responses (e.g., sales or newsletter subscriptions), experts like Zinger suggest that they can find their best results via a paid search campaign. On the other hand, SEO usually provides the cheapest and most effective way to drive a high volume of relevant impressions and clicks for marketers and ad agencies that can allocate the necessary time and effort to build and maintain content on their sites. Therefore, you might want to consider running a combination of both tactics and keep the "dialogue" between them. For example, complement the best performing paid search keywords (that have very little competition from other CPC campaigns) with SEO, and, conversely, complement high-quality, organic keywords with paid search advertising.

Unique Opportunities for Spanish Search

"Spanish SEO continues to be an opportunity in and of itself, compared to SEO in other languages such as English and Chinese," says Zinger. There are fewer Spanish sites in comparison with other languages, so competition tends to be lower.

Once you have optimized your website code and content to comply with search engine guidelines, focus on building fresh and relevant content. Find external sources to spread the word, hopefully linking back to your website. "One of the most successful tactics to do this is called "Link-baiting." It consists of creating content that appeals to people strongly enough that they link to it from their own websites, social network profiles, and so forth," says Zinger. The best place to do this is with local bloggers who can feature your valuable links and content for their readers.

Searching in English and Spanish

U.S. Hispanics sometimes search in English for the same reasons they read books, watch TV, or choose to communicate in English. It just makes sense in their day-to-day lives. U.S. Hispanics and many Latin Americans notice that there's a wider array of content online in English than in Spanish. Hence, when they search for a specific topic or something that is particularly hard to find, they might switch their search queries to English. For the time being, it's wise to offer both English and Spanish content.

Experts from Google and Yahoo! suggest buying keywords in both English and Spanish for reaching both English-dominant and Spanish-dominant U.S. Hispanics. This facilitates easy switching between the two languages for second-generation Hispanics who are comfortable in both languages. Google offers suggestions for how to best use search to reach U.S. Hispanics:

- U.S. Hispanics search in both languages so a mixture of both languages is key.
- Try different creative in different metropolitan areas.
- Use a Spanish-language landing page for the Spanish keywords just as you do for English-language keywords.

- Include accented and unaccented keywords.
- Experiment with Spanish variations of words from different parts of Latin America.
- Try using elements of Spanish and English in the same creative.

Recommendations for Great Search Engine Optimization (SEO)

- Research what users search for in your particular product category, determine their popularity, and evaluate the competition for each keyword.
- Choose the keywords and phrases that best correlate to your product and present the best opportunity for boosting search engine rankings.
- Analyze your website's content relative to those keywords.
- Change or add website content to better correspond to users searches, connecting you more directly with their wants and needs.
- Change, or optimize, the website code, page design, or site structure to make your website more "findable."
- Request links from other like-minded websites, press or bloggers.
- Integrate store or distributor listings on services like Google Maps that connect each address with a location on a map.
- Measure how those changes have improved visitor levels, time spent on your site, and overall marketing metrics.

Multilingual, International SEO

In an article on the website *Search Engine Land,* Andy Atkins-Krüger wrote that international website owners now realize that they have to coordinate translation and SEO activities. They have challenged their localization providers to manage SEO for them. By default, Internet marketing now brings together the SEO and localization industries that never worked together before. When you optimize your international sites for search, you should buy local domains in each market, host domains with local URL extensions in each country where you do business, culturally customize your content, and research and buy country-specific keywords.

It's surprising how few companies optimize their international, multilingual sites for search engines. In an article on the website *Multilingual Search* (February 12, 2010), Atkins-Krüger noted that, according to Google, 12,100 people search for the phrase "website translation" while only 1,000 search for "International SEO" on a monthly basis. "By my reckoning, that roughly means that only 8 percent of people who translate their website bother at any point to either consider SEO or buy a service for it. Is that possible? Far more people translate than employ any kind of SEO," says Atkins-Krüger.

Lessons Learned

- Evaluate content development partners based on their reach and the quality of the content that they produce,
- Evaluate consumers' content needs based on the level of interactivity desired or access they want across platforms.
- Set up systems to localize and distribute your content across multiple websites and social networks to provide you with ease-of-delivery and control.
- Premium websites allow marketers greater control of where their ad runs, content integration, and sponsorship opportunities.
- Online ad networks enable marketers to quickly and efficiently gain reach and optimize campaigns at relatively low CPMs.
- Optimize your domestic and international Spanish-language websites by working with search specialists who understand localization and SEO best practices.
- Analyze keyword rankings for your niche and the best local, in-country sites to link to yours.
- U.S. Hispanics sometimes search in English because it makes sense in their day-to-day lives but also because there's a wider array of content online in English.

- Buy country-specific geo-targeted keywords (aka, paid search) in Spanish to drive traffic to your Spanish-language site.

- Give consumers only a few choices and you can empower them to feel good about their choices. Provide links (to separate pages) for consumers who require more detailed information so as not to muddy the water for the majority of consumers who want only a few choices.

Chapter 11

The Future Today:
Mobile Platforms en Español

MOBILE marketing and content show great promise in the future as many experts suggest that Latinos globally will first use the Internet on a mobile device. Even today, U.S. Hispanics significantly over-index in the consumption of mobile content. While an entire book could be dedicated to this subject, this chapter will outline the research that supports this trend and provide you with some basic mobile marketing techniques (e.g., texting, coupons, contests) as well as highlight emerging mobile applications to watch.

According to a white paper from the Hispanic ad agency, Dieste, and the Association of National Advertisers entitled *Online Marketing to the U.S. Hispanics*, 31 million U.S. Hispanics have a mobile phone, and by age 17, the penetration rate of wireless services among U.S. Hispanic teens is 78 percent. According to the results of the National Health Interview Survey (Janurary-June, 2009), Hispanic adults (28 percent) are more likely than non-Hispanic white adults (19 percent) or non-Hispanic black adults (21 percent) to live in cell phone–only households.

If we compare U.S. Hispanic users to the general market, using comScore's Mobilens data (March 2010), the propensity for U.S. Hispanics to adopt new technologies on mobile platforms is quite astonishing.

	General Market	U.S. Hispanics
Use a mobile browser	30%	48%
Use applications	35%	53%
Accessed search	14%	22%
Accessed social networking	12%	21%
Accessed entertainment news	8%	16%

Looking ahead, "For the forecast period of 2009-2013, Hispanics will be the growth engine for new wireless subscribers, and based on early observations they will also be heavier users of enhanced services," according to The Insight Research Corporation's report *U.S. Hispanic Use of Telecom Services 2009-2014.*

Mobile Marketing Techniques

Taking these insights into consideration, let's look at some effective ways to market to Hispanics on mobile platforms. One of the most successful ways to drive sales to retail stores or restaurants on mobile devices is to incorporate your brand into Google Maps. It is the leader in location-based content and advertising, where wireless users can get directions from point A to point B, view what a location looks like, and find nearby retail stores

This of course taps into the highly local, GPS-powered nature of cell phones. Many consumers who notice mobile-based, location-specific advertising actually visit the store advertised because of its proximity at the moment. In the H&R Block case study, we saw that one of the most popular features is "find an office," so be sure to integrate your stores' locations or distribution channels into mobile maps and applications with information in Spanish.

"With almost every Internet-enabled device being able to broadcast its position, local content providers will need to step up and enhance their offer to maximize the opportunity. This will open the game for many new local players that can present high value in their content," says Jonatan Zinger of ad agency Media 8. Marketers can become heroes by developing helpful and contextually relevant product and location information on mobile devices.

However basic the technology may seem, SMS marketing, (Short Messaging Service), represents an effective option with response rates as much as 10 times higher than web-based advertising. Nearly all of the world's mobile phones can send and receive an SMS messages, also known as text messages. Marketers often measure the effectiveness of SMS direct-response campaigns by employing sweepstakes, voting (e.g., *American Idol*), or trivia contests.

Product marketers can take advantage of mobile marketing techniques like working with couponing companies such as Cellfire or developing branded entertainment content. Specifically, in the highly personal, mobile world, marketers find that delivering valuable content in exchange for consumers opting-in to receive marketing messages works well. For example, Starbucks can offer consumers a free cup of coffee in exchange for their response to a survey via SMS. Or cell phone service providers could offer consumers a free ringtone in exchange for receiving targeted ads on their mobile devices.

QR code (short for "quick response") and 2D barcode providers like JagTag allow consumers to request and receive on-demand digital content via SMS from a brand's print ads, out-of-home, point-of-sale, packaging, or physical stores. This presents an interesting option for making a longer lasting connection with consumers who can then access product demos, promotions, coupons, branded entertainment, subscriptions or notifications.

Bar code scanning service providers like RedLaser by Occipital enable mobile phone users to scan bar codes and receive corresponding product information. Stickybits is a social variation of RedLaser where users can attach or associate photos, videos, music, text, and PDFs to any barcode and see what others have associated with that very same product. In addition, Google has developed its mobile image search product, Google Goggles, which enables users to take photos of barcodes or images and look up more information about the product on their mobile devices.

There are some simple rules that you can follow to develop successful mobile campaigns. First, deliver useful, valuable content to consumers based on users' preselected interests from their opt-in information. Second, serve relevant offers, discounts, or ads based on that same opt-in information. Third, don't spam users with mass SMS messages or banners. For example, don't send subscribers country music ringtones if they like alternative music.

Teaching English on Mobile Phones

One company that reaches out to first-generation Hispanics via cell phones is Austin, Texas–based edioma, which offers English-language mini-courses on mobile phones. Larry Upton, edioma's founder and president, calls what edioma offers "enabling technology" that facilitates Hispanics' assimilation into U.S. society while at the same time offering a meaningful platform for sponsors to reach out to Hispanics.

The company provides a formula that other content providers and sponsors can copy in a mobile environment: offer customizable, user-controlled, learning-based content in short chunks via mobile phones for free in exchange for consumers watching targeted advertising. Opt-in data provided by consumers such as gender, age, language-preference, and location (when GPS capability exists within the handset) offers significant consumer insights for sponsors.

It launched its first retail product in July 2010 where Hispanics can download and purchase its "edigo" mobile phrase kits for situational language instruction. Each kit contains 50 context-specific phrases for use on the job, at the bank, while shopping, or visiting the doctor with vocabulary that appears on the cell screen. The corresponding pronunciations can be heard on the headset. Some of edioma's offerings are sponsor-funded kits. For example, a financial services language kit could be sponsored by a major bank. In addition, edioma launched a pilot program with 7-Eleven where it teaches its counter clerks to speak better Spanish via custom edigo phrase kits, to be used in the retail sales environment.

Some additional companies to keep your eye on in the Hispanic mobile world include Novebox which streams "TV" clips of telenovelas and celebrities to mobile phones; VoodooVox, which delivers in-call content and advertising while consumers are on hold when calling 1-800 numbers; 1(800)-HISPANO, a free information center for Hispanics, providing them with the necessary tools to make better decisions; and media providers like Telemundo or Univision.

Some other general market mobile companies to keep an eye on include mobile game providers like Greystripe that embed ads into games like Scrabble on the iPhone or Blackberry, where each player logs in to play from his or her respective phone, and an ad appears every time the player turns the game over to his or her fellow player; alternative cell phone provider like Virgin Mobile's "Sugar Mama" program that provides teens an opportunity to earn free cell phone minutes in exchange for watching web-based "fund my phone" advertising messages; and mobile payment companies like MPower Mobile, Boku, PayPal, and Square

Expansion into Latin America

Mobile Internet access will be key to any company targeting Latin American wireless subscribers, as 70 percent-plus of all first-time Internet experiences in Latin America are via mobile, according to Larry Upton of edioma.

"Across Latin America we see an extremely high reach of social networking on mobile devices. Combine this reach with the fact that this same category of content is one of the main drivers of mobile Internet adoption amongst young people around the world, and one can only assume a big future is on the way," says Alex Banks, VP, Latin America for ComScore.

Banks adds that, as Latin Americans move about around the world, content like family photos and birthday wishes can be easily shared on cell phones. "Publishers around the world should do what they can to embrace social media as a way to build their international audience in both the short and long term," he says.

One application that takes advantage of that is Chat del Mundo, which connects Latino mobile users through carriers in the U.S., Mexico, Venezuela, Argentina, Chile, Ecuador, Colombia, Panama, and Spain. Jumbuck Entertainment, its parent company, launched Chat Del Mundo to enable Spanish-speaking consumers to keep in touch with friends and family or connect with people who share similar interests via their mobile phones. Users can enter public or private chat rooms or with one specific member. Some of the most popular features include the "International Chats," where users enter chat rooms labeled with a flag for each country. Members in Mexico or of Mexican origin can chat in one room together. Brian Milton, Jumbuck's SVP, says that many U.S. Hispanics use this as one of their main ways to keep in touch with family and friends because of the low cost of $2 per month.

Lessons learned

- Hispanics will drive growth among new wireless subscribers, especially since they over-index for using services like using mobile applications as well as accessing social networks and entertainment news.
- Incorporate your retail stores or restaurants on mobile devices via Google Maps with GPS-enabled applications and information in Spanish.
- SMS marketing, or text messages, often deliver response rates as much as 10 times higher than web-based advertising and may employ promotional techniques such as sweepstakes, voting, or trivia contests.
- In the highly personal, mobile world, marketers find that delivering valuable content (ringtones, applications, wallpaper, etc) in exchange for consumers opting-in to receive marketing messages works well.
- Bar code scanning mobile applications empower consumers to find corresponding prices, product information, promotions or even comparison shop and locate out-of-stock items in nearby stores.
- Marketers and publishers alike can attract Latinos around the world by incorporating social media components into digital media campaigns as a way to build their audiences.

Promoting American Family Insurance on Mobile Platforms

By Jose A. Rivera
Web Experience Manager
American Family Insurance

Expanding mobile offerings to U.S. Hispanics is extremely encouraging as research shows that adoption rates for new technology and mobility trend higher when compared with the general market. Hispanics spend more than other segments of the population on fee-based mobile services such as mobile web, texting, mobile TV, and downloading content. Marketers view this as a great opportunity because of the potential to target mobile consumers on a one-to-one basis. In contrast, family members often share home computers. Using information about an individual's user behavior, navigation patterns, and media consumption opens the door for effective targeting that goes beyond geographic area or language. In the future, data captured on a mobile device may allow marketers to create predictive models based on data consumption, sites visited, mobile purchases, and social sharing that will enable mobile media placements for cents on the dollar.

WAP Website

Consumers can access Amfam.com via any web-enabled mobile, which allows us to optimize our site to the specifications of a user's devices. We do this to offer a good experience regardless of the type of screen the consumer uses. We also optimize our web tools with options for "find an agent," "file a claim," "view claim status," "my account," "online billing," and "request a quote" to use on all mobile devices. Our WAP site also includes product information and descriptions. Late in 2010, we will have launched the features described here in Spanish so that users accessing *amfamlatino.com* from a mobile device will automatically be re-routed to the optimized, mobile version of the site. In addition, we enable mobile advertising on our pages. This allows us to insert banners on any page to inform customers and prospects. Banners may promote new products, provide corporate information relevant to policyholders, and the latest mobile applications available for the user's device that has been detected by our ad serving system.

SMS Marketing

We strategically use texting in our advertising campaigns by including alerts to customers, event platforms, and value-added offerings. American Family Insurance owns short codes in both English and Spanish. With our short code "SEGURO," or "insurance" in English, we use in-language keywords to reach out to Spanish speaking prospects and customers with all of our offerings. Our advertising campaigns include calls to action for users to text us a specific keyword in order to find an agent, get a quote, or opt-in for more information about our products and services. We integrate our SMS marketing programs into our call center systems and so our well-trained staff is able to respond and transition from one channel to another including text messages, emails, or phone calls. Consumers can opt-in to receive text messages regarding billing alerts, due dates, payment confirmations, claims status updates and changes made by the agent. We also offer value-added text messages that alert our current customers about severe weather conditions. If the weather service issues a warning in the area of registered opt-in policyholders, we can send them a free text message alerting them of the potential danger. When a tornado appears, we send the message via a phone call instead of a text message to make sure everyone is safe and sound with such short notice.

Conclusion

As I finish this book in the summer of 2010, it is interesting to note that two companies have already followed the marketing leaders featured in *Latino Link*.

The insurance provider, Aflac, unveiled an interactive Spanish-language, culturally relevant website for Hispanic consumers. Aflac's press release reads, "Among the many interactive features, the site includes a special section 'Nuestras Historias' (Our Stories) featuring Aflac agents telling stories of their own success selling Aflac in the Hispanic market as well as the latest Spanish-language commercials."

Fox News announced the launch of FoxNewsLatino.com, which features breaking news, politics, economic, and lifestyle stories that impact the Latino community. The site features videos in both English and Spanish, and includes reports from the U.S. as well as Central America, South America, and the Caribbean. Fox News noticed that about a third of the country will be of Latino heritage by 2050, so it thought that the time was right to launch a site for this audience.

In conclusion, let's think about how we make our online content efforts successful through the eyes of Fernando (this little guy in the photo). He has mastered the art of walking and, of course, has just graduated to running. What did it take to get here? How many times did he fall down along the way? Launching and localizing your Spanish-language digital content is similar in that you may fall down as it's always a work in progress but that will lead you to success.

Define your goals and start taking those baby steps to get there. Don't delay the learning process. The companies featured in our case studies—American Family Insurance, Best Buy, Ford, H&R Block, and Lexicon Marketing—all share a few things in common: They made a commitment to reaching the Hispanic audience and kept at it. They started early and acquired the necessary skills to communicate to the growing Latino community online and offline. In the years ahead, as this audience grows in importance, your persistence will pay off.

Appendix

Research

AS A PART of the research for this book, in April 2010, I sent out two separate surveys to marketing experts in media sales, media planning, localization, product/brand management and academia. The first survey went to respondents in the U.S. Hispanic market and the second went to Mexico. Each was customized to its respective country and points of view. For example, the survey in Mexico contained a number of questions about the survey takers' own online search and shopping habits, which confirmed my conclusions in Chapter 4 about how much middle and upper class Mexicans shop in the U.S.

Overall, the surveys accomplished my goal of verifying the accuracy of my conclusions made in the book, namely the pan-regionalization of Spanish-language online media and the need for better-localized content strategies. You can see from the answers both from the U.S. Hispanic market and Mexico that there is a need for more content and information online in Spanish.

In the case of the U.S. Hispanic market, the vast majority of experts surveyed, 79 percent, think that universal Spanish "makes the most sense on the worldwide web." But, as we saw in Chapter 7, universal Spanish makes the most sense from the outset because that it is the cheapest to implement. But often, because of local terms and vocabulary, the country-specific Spanish ends up being the best understood by local audiences.

Following are the results of the two surveys.

I sent the first survey via email to 330 professionals in the U.S. Hispanic marketing and advertising industry. Fifty-five people responded, answering 16 questions, which made for a 17 percent response rate.

I work in . . .
  Brand management: 23.3%
  Media planning/agency executive: 32.6%
  Product management: 2.3%
  Digital media sales: 25.6%
  Localization/translation: 16.3%

Are you bilingual?
  Yes, I speak English and Spanish: 90.9%
  No, I only speak English: 5.5%
  I'd like to learn Spanish: 3.6%

Is there a need for more content in Spanish on the Internet?
  Yes: 87.0%
  No: 5.6%
  Don't know: 7.4%

In a recent AOL Latino study of online Hispanics, only 3% of respondents said that "I trust the Spanish-language site more." Do you think this is because of:
  Lack of content in Spanish: 9.4%
  Poorly translated web sites: 24.5%
  Bilingual Hispanics prefer English: 20.8%
  All of the above: 41.5%
  Don't know/Haven't read the study: 3.8%
  Other (please specify): 6 comments

Do you buy keywords to promote your Spanish-language (or a client) site?
  Yes: 46.3%
  No: 33.3%
  Don't know: 7.4%
  No opinion: 13.0%

If yes, what language do you buy keywords in?
  English: 8.7%
  Spanish: 17.4%
  Both: 37.0%
  I'm not involved in this decision: 37.0%

In your opinion, why do Hispanics search in both English and Spanish?
  There isn't enough content in Spanish: 14.8%
  They are bilingual: 24.1%
  Both a and b: 53.7%
  They mostly search in Spanish: 0.0%
  Don't know: 3.7%
  No comment: 3.7%

In your opinion, why do Hispanics visit sites from Latin America?

To keep in touch with their home country: 51.0%

They end up on foreign sites because of search engine results or what's shared on social media sites: 7.8%

Both a and b: 41.2%

What type of Spanish do you think makes the most sense for the worldwide web?

Universal (neutral) Spanish: 79.2%

Latin American Spanish: 7.5%

Country-specific/regional Spanish: 13.2%

Do you think that social commenting enables publishers/marketers to use universal Spanish and then customize a site or add reviews in the Spanish (or even Spanglish) that is natural to the user?

Yes: 57.7%

No: 9.6%

Don't know: 26.9%

No comment: 5.8%

Is online media becoming more pan-regionalized?

Yes: 52.7%

No: 18.2%

Don't know: 27.3%

No comment: 1.8%

Will online media become more local in nature?

Yes: 65.5%

No: 20.0%

Don't know: 14.5%

How do CPMs (cost per thousand) or CPCs (cost per click) in the Hispanic market compare to the general market?

Higher: 23.6%

Lower: 41.8%

Same: 9.1%

Don't know: 25.5%

Will marketers be more or less likely to launch Spanish-language web sites and online campaigns in the future?

Yes, more likely: 81.8%

No, less likely: 10.9%

Don't know: 5.5%

No comment: 1.8%

Do you think there will be an increase in Hispanic online advertising in the next two years?

Yes: 92.7%

No: 7.3%

Does your organization outsource Hispanic content production, creative development or campaign management to Latin America where labor rates are generally much lower?

> Yes: 43.6%
> No: 50.9%
> Don't know: 3.6%
> No comment: 1.8%

I sent the second survey, in Spanish, via email to 260 professionals in the Mexican marketing and advertising industry. Forty-six people responded, answering the 23 questions, which provided for an 18 percent response rate. Following are the responses to that survey, translated from Spanish into English.

I work in . . .

> Media sales: 16.1%
> Media planning/agency executive: 29%
> Product management: 12.9%
> Brand management: 12.9%
> Marketing and media consulting: 41.9%

Are you bilingual?

> Yes, I speak English: 95.7%
> No, I don't: 0%
> I'd like to learn: 4.3%

When you use a search engine, do you search in Spanish or English as well?

> Only Spanish: 2.2%
> Both in Spanish and English: 95.7%
> Spanish and another language: 2.2%

What search engine do you prefer?

> Google: 89.1%
> Bing: 4.3%
> Yahoo!: 2.2%
> All of the above: 4.3%

In your opinion, is there more content available on the Internet in English than in Spanish?

> Yes: 84.8%
> No: 8.7%
> Haven't thought about it: 6.5%

Does content availability affect your search engine usage behavior?

> Yes: 67.4%
> No: 32.6%

Does it matter if results are from Mexican sites?

> Yes: 70.5%
> No, I only care if I get the answer that I want, in Spanish: 29.5%

Do you visit U.S. or foreign web sites?

> In Spanish: 6.7%
> In English: 11.1%
> Both Spanish and English: 48.9%
> I don't care where sites are based: 31.1%
> No: 2.2%

If yes to question number 8, what kinds of content do you like to visit?

> Sites related to my profession: 21.4%
> News: 9.5%
> Entertainment: 7.1%
> Product research: 2.4%
> Financial/investment: 0%
> All of the above: 50%
> Not applicable: 9.5%

Do you plan or sell digital advertising in the United States?

> Yes: 30.4%
> No: 56.5%
> Not applicable: 13%

How do you see the opportunity to expand your business in the U.S. in the Hispanic market?

> Yes, on the Internet there aren't any borders: 76.1%
> No, it's a different market: 15.2%
> Not applicable: 8.7%

Do you make purchases online in Mexico or the U.S.?

> Often: 30.4%
> Sometimes: 52.2%
> Rarely: 10.9%
> Never: 6.5%

If yes, what sites do you make purchases on?

> Mexican sites (e.g. MercadoLibre): 4.5%
> U.S. sites (e.g. Amazon): 34.1%
> All of the above: 54.5%
> None: 6.8%

Have you ever made a purchase from Mexico and had it shipped to a U.S. address (family member, hotel, etc)?

> Yes: 44.4%
> No: 55.6%

Have you visited the U.S. in the last three years?

> Yes: 76.1%
> No: 17.4%
> I plan to: 4.3%
> Not applicable: 2.2%

Do you go to the U.S. for work or pleasure?

> Work: 8.7%
> Pleasure: 28.3%
> Both: 50%
> Not applicable: 13%

If yes, how often do you visit?

> Less than once per year: 10.9%
> Once a year: 21.7%
> Twice a year: 21.7%
> Three times a year: 34.8%
> Not applicable: 10.9%

Do you go shopping when you visit the U.S.?

> Yes: 88.9%
> No: 11.1%

If yes, do you plan your trip around shopping?

> Always: 13.3%
> Sometimes: 42.2%
> Never: 33.3%
> Not applicable: 11.1%

What items do you buy?

> Consumer electronics: 15.9%
> Clothing: 40.9%
> Luxury goods (watches, perfume): 0%
> Furniture: 0%
> Liquor and food: 0%
> All of the above: 29.5%
> Not applicable: 13.6%

How long do you typically stay for?

> Less than two days: 0%
> 2-5 days: 52.2%
> 5 or more days: 34.8%
> Not applicable: 13%

What is your typical shopping expenditure per trip?

> Less than $200 USD: 2.2%
> $200 -$500 USD: 19.6%
> $500-$1000 USD: 26.1%
> More than $1000 USD: 39.1%
> Not applicable: 13%

Do you plan or sell digital media in Mexico for Mexicans that shop in the United States?

> Yes: 31.1%
> No: 53.3%
> Not applicable: 15.6%

Bibliography

Books

Anderson, Benedict, *Imagined Communities: Reflections on the Origin and Spread of Nationalism* (New Edition), Verso, 2006.

Anderson, Chris *The Long Tail: Why the Future of Business Is Selling Less of More,* Hyperion, 2006.

Benitez, Cristina. *Latinization: How Latino Culture is Transforming the U.S.* Ithaca, NY: Paramount Market Publishing, Inc., 2007.

Cancela, Jose *The Power of Business en Espanol: 7 Fundamental Keys to Unlocking the Potential of the Spanish-Language Hispanic Market,* Rayo, 2007.

DePalma, Donald A. *Business Without Borders: A Strategic Guide to Global Marketing.* Globa Vista Press, 2004.

Friedman, Thomas L. *The World is Flat: a Brief History of the Twenty-First Century.* Farrar, Straus and Giroux, 2006.

Gladwell, Malcolm. *The Tipping Point: How Little Things Can Make a Big Difference.* Back Bay Books, 2002.

Halvorson, Kristina. *Content Strategy for the Web* Pearson Education, Inc. and New Riders, 2010.

Korzenny, Felipe *Hispanic Marketing: A Cultural Perspective*, Butterworth-Heinemann, 2005.

McLuhan, Marshall and Lapham, Lewis *Understanding Media: The Extensions of Man Understanding Media: The Extensions of* Man The MIT Press, 1994.

Singh, Nitish and Arun Pereira. *The Culturally Customized Website: Customizing Web Sites for the Global Marketplace.* Butterworth-Heinemann, 2005.

Yunker, John. *Beyond Borders: Web Globalization Strategies.* New Riders Press, 2002.

White Papers, Research Reports and Magazine Articles

Abasto Magazine, Juan Tornoe "Regionalized vs. Walter Cronkite Spanish," March 2010, P62.

AdAge Hispanic Fact Pack 2009, July 27, 2009, Crain Communications, Inc.

AMIPCI (Asociación Mexicana de Internet) - Hábitos de los Usuarios de Internet en México, 2009.

AMIPCI Estudio de Comercio Electrónico 2009.

Association of National Advertisers (ANA) Online Marketing to the U.S. Hispanic, written by Dieste.

Byte Level Research, "Seven Habits of Highly Successful Global Web Sites."

Byte Level Research, "The Art of the Global Gateway, 2006."

Byte Level Research, "The Web Globalization Report Card—2010."

Byte Level Research, "Going Global with Geolocation: How companies are using geolocation to improve navigation for Web users around the world," 2008.

Common Sense Advisory, "Leaving La Vida Loca. Analysis of the Opportunity," 2004.

Common Sense Advisory, "Online Retail Not Latino-Friendly. Few U.S. Web Retailers Service Hispanic Market," 2004.

Common Sense Advisory, "Reaching America's e-Latinos Otra Vez. How Well Do America's Top Online Retailers Reach Out to Latinos?" 2007.

Common Sense Advisory, "Developing Multicultural Websites. How to Meet the Needs of Domestic Market Minority and Ethnic Populations," 2007.

Common Sense Advisory, "The Top 40 Global Online Brands. Best and Worst Practices in Website Globalization," 2009.

eBay 2008 and 2009 Annual Reports.

eMarketer, Mexico Online Overview, 2007.

eMarketer, Hispanics Online: Demographics and Media Usage, May 2010.

eMarketer, Age of Internet users in Mexico – INEGI 2007 – "National survey about the availability and use of information technologies in the home" (Bar Graph).

eMarketer, "How Much Choice Do Consumers Want?" March, 2008.

eMarketer, "Hispanics go online for trusted info," Feb. 2010.

Ethnologue: Languages of the World, 2009, SIL International.

ESIGMA, economic analysis of Mexican population.

Forrester Research, "How To Measure ROI For Spanish-Language US Sites," Jan. 2009.

Forrester Research, Technographics® Survey Highlights: "eCommerce Landscape In Mexico And Brazil," Dec. 2009.

Forrester Research, "Social Media Is Mainstream For Online Hispanics," March 2010.

Google Mexico online retail study, September 2009.

Haddad, Ghassan, The Facebook Translation Model, presentation from Localization World Conference, 2009.

Hispanic Cyberstudy. "Marketing to the web's most rapidly growing population." Commissioned by AOL and conducted by Cheskin, 2010.

Interactive Advertising Bureau (IAB), "U.S. Latinos Online: A Driving Force." (white paper) ww.iab.net/us_latinos

IAB Mexico & Price Waterhouse Coopers, 2009, "Estudio de Inversión Publicitaria en Internet en México-2009."

IAB Mexico & MillwardBrown, "Estudio de consumo de medios digitales en México," 2009.

IAB Spain & Price Waterhouse Coopers, "Estudio sobre la Inversion publicitaria en medios digitales," 2009.

Insight Research Corporation, "U.S. Hispanic Use of Telecom Services 2009-2014."

The International Shopping Traveler Study: Commissioned by Taubman Centers and Shop America Alliance LLC. In partnership with U.S. Department of Commerce Office of Travel & Tourism Industries Conducted by Mandala Research & Consulting, 2009.

Lionbridge, "Spanish Variants: What to offer?" April 2009.

Lionbridge, "Building a Global Web Strategy. Best Practices for Developing your International Online Brand," 2009.

Lionbridge, "Building Stronger Brands Around the World: A Guide to Effective Global Marketing," 2009.

Louisiana Tax Free Shopping (LTFS) Refund Center Data 2009.

MercadoLibre, Inc. Annual Report 2009.

Scarborough Research, "The Power of the Hispanic Consumer Online," 2008.

Selig Center for Economic Growth, "The Multicultural Economy," 2009.

Singh, Nitish. Lecture: Web Site Globalization, Step by Step: Global Navigation and Web Usability. John Cook School of Business at Saint Louis University, 2009.

Synovate and Greater Miami Convention & Visitors Bureau; "Visitor Profile and Economic Impact Study January-December 2008," May, 2009.

Tomas Rivera Policy Institute, "The Social Impact of Voice Over Internet Protocol Technology on Latinos," 2009.

Universal McCann, "Power To The People: Wave 4 Social Media Study," 2009.

U.S. Bureau of Transportation, border-crossing data between Mexico and United States, 2008.

Visa's Tourism Outlook: USA, June 2009.

Visa's US International Tourism Outlook, July 2008.

World Bank; Mexico World Bank Development Indicators. World Development Indicators database, September 2009.

World Bank, "Close to Home. The Development Impact of Remittances in Latin America Conducted by The International Bank for Reconstruction and Development," 2007.

Yorokobu magazine, "Sin mapa no hay tesoro," by Pedro Mujica, December 2009.

Online Articles and Resources

Arcos, Eduardo. Español más propio de Latinoamérica, 2009,
    http://eduardo.arcos.cc/2009/10/espanol-mas-propio-de-latinoamerica/

Banxico. Balanza de Pagos, Ingreso por Remesas.
    http://www.banxico.org.mx/SieInternet/consultarDirectorioInternetAction.
    do?accion=consultarCuadro&idCuadro=CE81&sector=1&locale=es

BBC Mundo, América Latina, líder en redes sociales by David Cuen, March 24, 2010

CBS News, Mexico Sees Record Drop in Remittances, Jan. 27. 2010.

CIA World Factbook. Country Comparison: Internet Hosts, 2009.

Internet World Stats, Spanish-Speaking Internet Usage Statistics

Internet World Stats, Internet Usage Statistics

Internet World Stats, Top languages on the Internet

Multilingual Search, Website Translation or International SEO? 92% of Website Translators Ignore SEO? by Andy Atkins-Krüger, Feb 12, 2010

New York Times, "In Argentina, a Camera and a Blog Make a Star," March 13, 2009

Pew Hispanic Center, US Hispanic Population by County (Map).
    http://pewhispanic.org/states/population/

Portada, Univision Launches New Digital Advertising and Publishing Network, Dec. 1, 2009

Molina, Nathalie. (Oct. 2008). What is language for multilinguals?
    http://globalmisfit.com/2008/10/07/what-is-language/

Instituto Cervantes Biblioteca Severo Ochoa.(Sep. 2009) I Concurso de Microrrelatos.
    http://cervanteschicago.wordpress.com/2009/09/24/i-concurso-de-
    microrrelatos-de-la-biblioteca-severo-ochoa-del-instituto-cervantes-de-
    chicago/

Search Engine Land, *Is International Social Media Marketing Just Too Difficult?*, Andy Atkins-Krüger, http://searchengineland.com/is-international-social-media-marketing-just-too-difficult-35285

TechCrunch – Facebook translation http://techcrunch.com/2009/09/29/facebook-spreads-its-crowdsourced-translations-across-the-web-and-the-world/

Wikipedia. Money Remittances to Latam http://en.wikipedia.org/wiki/Remittance#Latin_America_and_the_ Caribbean

Wikipedia. Hispanophone world map http://en.wikipedia.org/wiki/File:Hispanophone_world_map.png

Wikipedia. Top natively spoken languages in the world http://en.wikipedia.org/wiki/List_of_languages_by_number_of_native_ speakers

Index

About the Author

JOE KUTCHERA is a leading speaker and consultant on reaching Hispanics and Latin Americans online, bringing over 11 years of interactive sales and marketing experience to his clients. Previously, Joe launched ContextWeb's Spanish-language ad network for U.S. Hispanics and opened its Mexico City office as its Director of Spanish-Language Markets.

During his nine-year tenure at Time Warner, Joe built web properties such as Warner Bros. Online, ThisOldHouse.com, CNNMoney, and CNNExpansion. During his last two years at the company, Joe started the digital ad sales team for Grupo Editorial Expansion in Mexico City, acquired by Time Inc in 2005, launching the websites CNNExpansion, Quien.com and Chilango.com.

You can read Joe's columns about best practices for reaching U.S. Latinos online on MediaPost and Portada. Joe has spoken at conferences and universities in the U.S., Spain, and Mexico about the consumer behavior of Hispanics and Latin Americans online as well as how to develop and localize content for them. In addition, Joe has written for iMedia, Life & Style and Chilango magazines as well as the Milwaukee Journal Sentinel, his hometown newspaper.

Joe has served as a board member for the Interactive Advertising Bureau (IAB) Mexico and as a member of the Hispanic Committee for the IAB in the U.S. He has a BA from Macalester College and an MBA from Fordham University. He currently lives in Chicago and has lived in Mexico City, New York, Prague and San Juan, Puerto Rico. You can read his blog and share a downloadable sample chapter of this book with your friends at: JoeKutchera.com.